LETTER

TO

THE HONORABLE

THE BOARD OF TRUSTEES

OF THE

UNIVERSITY OF MISSISSIPPI.

BY

FREDERICK A. P. BARNARD, LL.D.,

PRESIDENT OF THE UNIVERSITY.

OXFORD:
UNIVERSITY OF MISSISSIPPI.
1858.

TRUSTEES

OF THE

University of Mississippi.

LETTER.

University of Mississippi, March 15, 1858.

To the Members of
The Board of Trustees of the University of Mississippi:—

Gentlemen:—

Certain matters of weight relating to the system of education and instruction pursued in this institution, have long appeared to the undersigned to require, when the fitting moment should arrive, your deliberate and careful attention. The undersigned has therefore, for the last two or three years, constantly cherished the purpose to lay these matters before you, so soon as the internal condition of the University, in regard to its instrumental means and material conveniences for imparting instruction of the highest order, should have begun to approximate to that degree of perfection at which you have been so steadily and perseveringly aiming. That period, accelerated by the provision made by the Legislature of the State, at its session of 1856, in response to your appeal, appears now to have arrived;

and there remains no longer any reason why the consideration of the matters to which allusion has just been made should be any longer deferred.

In the beginning, it may seem proper to explain for what reason the undersigned has chosen to adopt the present form of communication with the members of your honorable body, instead of awaiting the period of your stated annual meeting, and embodying the topics here discussed into the usual official report of the head of the University. Were these topics such as to call only for ordinary legislation, this latter course would undoubtedly be the most appropriate. But involving, as they do, a consideration of the expediency of introducing into the arrangement and division of the subjects embraced in the educational course already existing, changes of some considerable moment, it is eminently desirable that they should be made subjects of more mature and deliberate reflection, than the usually brief duration of your annual sessions allows; and it will no doubt be considered by yourselves also an advantage to be able to make them a subject of consultation with the friends of education among the people of the State, before you shall be called on to pass upon them your final judgment. These reasons have determined the undersigned to express his views in the form of a circular letter, issued long enough before the period of your annual assembling, to enable you to bring to the meeting opinions unembarrassed by hesitation or doubt.

It need hardly be called to your attention that the educational world has long been agitated by the question, whether the American college system has not failed to keep pace with the intellectual advancement of the age in which we live. So large have been the conquests of mind, especially in the field of physical science, during the present century, that a much more considerable amount of positive knowledge is now expected of a liberally educated man, than was the case when the system originated. Such knowledge it is demanded that the colleges shall impart; yet the popular voice, in making this demand, disregards almost entirely the consideration that the college system, in its theory, contemplates not so much the communication of knowledge as the discipline and training of the intellectual powers. And the attempt to silence the importunity by holding up this consideration, is practically vain; for if the value of the knowledge and its necessity to the completeness of a finished education be admitted, the fact that it can nowhere be generally obtained if not in colleges, is always deemed a sufficient reply. It is therefore claimed that, however exclusive of all purposes but one may have been the original idea of the system, the condition of the world forbids that it should longer continue to be so. It is claimed that the necessity of the age requires of colleges, that they should no longer teach merely with the view, through the exercise of the mind upon the subjects taught, to develop the intellectual powers; but that, besides this, they should make knowledge itself, for its uses, the end of their teaching, and should therefore, teach much more than was esteemed necessary—more, in fact, than existed to be taught—a century ago. The colleges have tacitly admitted the justice of this claim. They have yielded to the urgency of a demand which they saw no means of resisting. They have adopted successively into their course, many studies which have no especial disciplinary value, and many which, fifty years ago, were not regarded as having any proper place there. In some instances this has undoubtedly been done in the sincere hope of enlarging their usefulness; in others, through the apprehension of a loss of public patronage, without; and in others still, merely from a spirit of imitation. But, in the mean time, the period covered by the entire course has remained unaltered. Much more in quantity is nominally taught, but no greater length of time is devoted to the teaching. The conclusion is therefore irresistible, either that the original design of the college is no longer perfectly secured, or that the additional subjects are very inadequately taught, or—a supposition more probable than either—that both these disadvantages exist together.

That the efficiency of the college course, considered as a system of intellectual discipline, has been impaired by the additions which have been made to it, is a point which need hardly be argued; for it is self-evident that if it were tolerably well adjusted in the beginning, it must now be excessively overloaded. Nor need we seek to fortify the argument by insisting on the comparatively imperfect adaptation of many of the added studies to the purposes of mental training; since, whatever may be their character in this respect, it is impossible that they should be productive of beneficial effects except in proportion as they can be mastered within the time allotted to them. However true it may be that the mind is improved and strengthened by the processes through which it is informed, it is certainly not reasonable to look for such results from those hasty or confused operations which fail clearly to inform it. It is only those efforts of the understanding which terminate in a consciousness of real mastery over a subject of thought, which, in an educational point of view, are truly useful; and it is certain that the instruction given in colleges is, in this sense, just so far thrown away as it leads to the formation of superficial, vague, or shadowy notions of truth.

Should the conjecture be hazarded that the evil here charged upon a system, is possibly due only to the inefficiency of men—that if the knowledge imparted by our colleges upon many of the subjects which they professedly teach, is actually imperfect and vague, the fault is to be ascribed to want of zeal or ability in the teachers, and not to the nature of things—it appears to the undersigned that the injustice of such an imputation may easily be made to appear. For this purpose it will be quite sufficient to consider in detail the various subjects in science and letters which the course embraces, and to compare the aggregate with the limited time which is allotted to their study. If we reduce this time to days or weeks, and then divide it by the total number of subjects, the result will be to indicate, of course, what is the average space allotted to each particular subject within the four years to which the course extends. Inasmuch, however, as the pressure is chiefly on the two latter years, and as it is to these that the encroachments made by modern additions have been principally confined, it will be by considering them apart from the earlier years, that the disproportion between matter and time will be made most striking.

Now, if we examine the curriculum of study as laid down in the prospectus of the University of Mississippi, we shall find that, during the Junior and Senior years, we profess to give instruction in four languages besides the English—two of them introduced during these years for the first time—and that to these subjects we add the History of Ancient Literature, Ethics, Metaphysics, Political Economy, Natural Philosophy, Astronomy, Civil Engineering, Chemistry, Mineralogy, Geology, International Law, and Constitutional Law—in all sixteen subjects, most or all of them of great extent. The time allotted to the study of these, deduction being made for examinations, amounts to two sessions of forty weeks each, in all eighty weeks; which allows, upon an average, five weeks to each study. But if we consider that several of the titles here enumerated are general titles, embracing under them several subordinate but quite distinct subjects, it will be immediately evident that even the small average of time above stated must be still further reduced. Several of the subjects of Natural Philosophy cohere so loosely as hardly to be united except by a common name. Astronomy has three or four ramifications, broadly distinct. General Chemistry has two large sub-divisions; and applied Chemistry, as related to metallurgy, to manufactures, to medicine, to agriculture, and to analysis, several more. Geology is descriptive, theoretic, and economical; and Paleontology, an allied science, has attained a position almost independent. Civil Engineering is a mixed science, involving many applications of mathematical principles and physical laws, and in addition to these, the gathered results of much actual observation and experiment, and the practical rules of several mechanic arts. Should we, therefore, endeavor to sub-divide the material embraced under the several titles drawn, as above, from the published programme of the University course, into portions each sufficiently differing from those with which it is associated to justify its distinct enumeration as a separate subject of study, we should obtain as a result a total of between thirty and forty; and by consequence, an allotment to each of little more than two weeks.

It is true that the system of instruction pursued in colleges, founded, as it is, on the principle of keeping the several faculties of the mind in proportionate and enarly simultaneous activity, requires that several of the studies above enumerated should be pursued together; so that no one of these subjects is actually dismissed in the short time which these calculations would assign to it. But it is no less true that, however long any one of them may continue to constitute a part of the daily employment of the student, it cannot actually, in the final aggregate, occupy a greater portion of his attention than the computation shows; or, at least, that if it *should* do so, the advantage could only be secured at the expense of the rest. This exhibit is, therefore, sufficient in itself to demonstrate that if there be superficiality in the attainments of the graduates of our colleges, this fault, or this evil, is not fairly chargeable to the instructors. It is the system itself which has become vitiated by the attempt to make it accomplish something inconsistent with its original design.

The evil has been the growth of years. It has accumulated by degrees almost imperceptible. Each successive addition has probably seemed inconsiderable to those who made it, but the united sum has become intolerable. Could it, in the nature of things, have been possible that a proposition should at any one time have been made for a sudden change from the system as it existed a century ago to the system of to-day, it is inconceivable that it should have been entertained by enlightened educators for a moment.

There can be no doubt that the views here presented have taken a strong hold of the minds of the friends of education throughout the United States. There can be no doubt of the existence of a disposition widely extended, to adopt some mode of relieving the course of undergraduate study in our colleges of some part of its excessive burthen. This has manifested itself in various ways. It has manifested itself, in some instances, in the introduction of parallel courses of study, as at Brown University, the University of Rochester, Union College, and partially at Harvard. It has manifested itself in attempts to throw open all the departments of learning to the choice of the undergraduate student, after the plan of the University of Virginia—an institution which has pursued this policy from the beginning; but this expedient, however apparently successful in that now celebrated seminary, has elsewhere usually entailed infinite annoyance, and not seldom disaster, upon those who have adopted it. It has manifested itself, again, in a manner more visibly productive of valuable results in the creation, in connection with some of our colleges, of extra-collegiate departments, devoted mainly to theoretic and practical science, and to the applications of Chemistry and Philosophy to the arts. And finally, it has manifested itself in the establishment, in a college which had previously presented but a single course of study terminating in the degree of Bachelor of Arts, of a second course, intended to commence where the first ends, and leading to the higher degree of Master of Arts.

This last mode of dealing with the case has long seemed to the undersigned to be the most judicious; and its adoption in this University has seemed to him to be the measure best adapted to increase the usefulness of the institution, while possessing the additional recommendation of at the same time elevating its character. It is a measure further recommended by the approval of very high authority, and by the precedent of some of the most distinguished institutions of learning in the country. The Southern Quarterly Review, in an article published in the spring of 1856—an article understood to be from the pen of the Rev. Dr. Thornwell, late the president of the College of South Carolina, a gentleman without a superior among Southern educators—points out precisely this mode of relieving our colleges of their burthen. In the re-arrangement of the system of instruction of Brown University, which took place in 1850, in accordance with the ably argued views of the eminent man then at the head of that institution—Dr. Wayland—a course of study for the Master's degree was introduced as a part of the new system. The University of Virginia, which permits to all its students to select their departments of study, makes, nevertheless, definite exactions of all who aspire to the degree of Bachelor of Arts; and much higher exactions of such as aim to proceed to the degree of Master. And during the past year, Columbia College, in the city of New York, one of the most wealthy institutions in the country, and also one of the earliest established, after a long period of deliberate inquiry and extensive correspondence with the most experienced friends of education throughout the United States, has instituted exactly the system which is here recommended.

The expediency of adopting a similar system here, cannot, therefore, be justly regarded as problematical. The system has, in effect, been already tried; and its adoption by the enlightened Board of Trustees of Columbia College, during the past year, with the results of experiment, and the approving opinions of the most competent authorities in the country before them, is evidence that it is in accordance with the exigencies of the case, and with the spirit of progress which characterizes the age.

It will probably be expected of the undersigned, not merely in general terms to suggest a division of the studies now pursued in college into two distinct and separate courses; but to specify particularly the subjects to be embraced by each,—or, where subjects are identical, the comparative extent which it is proposed to give to the corresponding studies in the two successive courses. The sub-graduate course may be defined by the very simple process of excluding from the curriculum of study as it stands at present, all those branches of science which are confessedly modern additions, and along with these, the modern languages. This course will, therefore, as re-constructed, embrace the English, Latin, and Greek languages, all the elementary branches of the pure Mathematics, the mechanical branches of Natural Philosophy, Logic, Rhetoric, the principles of Criticism, Moral and Mental Philosophy,

Composition, and Elocution. These several branches of study are to be pursued to something like the extent, and with something like the thoroughness contemplated in the earlier period of the history of our collegiate instruction. To these, it may not be thought improper to add, during the concluding year, succinct expository courses in Chemistry and the subjects of Natural Philosophy, not strictly mechanical; these topics being taught avowedly in outline only, and not as matters to be embraced in the examination for the Bachelor's degree. The design of this feature, if introduced, will be, in part, to vary to the student the interest of his daily occupations; but chiefly, by giving some slight foretaste of the nature of the subjects thus treated, to awaken in him a desire to enter upon the more thorough study of the same subjects in the higher department. The amount of time bestowed in this way need be but limited. Whatever is more than enough to secure the ends just mentioned, and especially the latter of them, is capable, during the period of the student's education here considered, of better occupation.

To the post-graduate department, may be turned over those branches of science and letters which are excluded from the former, and which are confessedly at present, but imperfectly taught; and the number of these may from time to time be increased, by adding new ones as the wants of the public and the growing resources of the University may demand or justify. Thus, it *may* immediately include Astronomy, Geology, Mineralogy, Chemistry, Natural Philosophy, Meteorology, Civil Engineering, the higher branches of the pure Mathematics, Greek and Roman Letters, the Modern Languages and their Literature, Political Economy, International Law, Constitutional Law, and the History of Philosophy; but it probably *will* include at first only such of this list as are most practical in their nature. As in creating this department, the design should be from the beginning, to build up here ultimately a University in the largest acceptation of that term, it is to be expected that, in the progress of years, schools of Agriculture, of Natural History, of Medical Science, of Civil and Political History, of Oriental Learning, and others, will be established as they shall appear to be needed; and that the existing School of Law will be strengthened by the addition of new professorships.

The instruction given in all the schools of this higher department is to proceed on the supposition that the student is familiar with every thing taught in the sub-graduate course, relating to the branches of study corresponding to those he is pursuing. Since, however, the design of the proposed change is to insure to the student a thorough and satisfactory acquaintance with extended and difficult subjects of knowledge, in regard to which the present system furnishes him only with indistinct and superficial notions, it is a feature of essential importance in the new plan, that every post-graduate student shall be perfectly free to choose the schools in which he will study; and that no one shall be obliged to study any thing which he does not choose. But since the degree of Master of Arts, if ever conferred, must have a certain significancy in order to be of value, it would be proper to adopt here such rules on this subject as exist in the University of Virginia, and to admit to the honor of this degree only those who have exhibited proficiency in a prescribed number and variety of schools. The Master's degree, moreover, should not be conferred upon any who have not been previously, either in this University or in some other, graduated as Bachelors of Arts. This regulation will have a favorable influence in encouraging young men to begin at the beginning, and to take the regular collegiate course, rather than to attempt the studies of the higher department without the important preliminary intellectual training.

The department ought, nevertheless, to be freely open to all who may wish to enter it, and who may have prepared themselves, either in schools or by private study, to avail themselves with profit of the opportunities it affords. But it should not undertake to *furnish* such preparation, since this would be to defeat its own object. With elementary instruction it should have nothing to do. But if any one, whether a graduate of a college or not, should desire to go thoroughly to the bottom of any subject which the University professes to teach, he should be free to pursue his object in this department, and should be furnished with every aid which books, and instruments, and competent teachers can afford. Thus, if it is the desire of any young man to obtain a satisfactory acquaintance with the applications of mathematical principles and physical truths to the art of construction, and with the accumulated results of observation and experiment in this important branch of practical science, let him come here and make, if he pleases, Civil Engineering his exclusive study, until such time as he may begin to feel some confidence in the value of the knowledge he shall have acquired. Or if his aim is to become a master of the art of Chemical Analysis, or of Chemistry as applied to Agriculture, let him have the opportunity to turn his attention with equal exclusiveness in that direction, and the assistance which may be necessary to enable him to attain the desired end. And so of the several other branches of letters and science which may be provided for in this higher department of the University—embracing in the *ultimate* design, of course, every possible subject of human learning or human investigation; let all be accessible to all applicants whose degree of intellectual advancement is such at the outset as to enable them to profit by the opportunities afforded.

It is, of course, assumed that the students in this higher department will be in earnest in the pursuit of knowledge; an assumption which cannot safely be made of the body of the under-graduates of our colleges. Nor is it difficult to find reasons for a fact of so general observation. One of these is, doubtless, the immaturity of the youthful student himself; in consequence of which he is yet to learn both the importance of mental culture, and the value of positive knowledge. Another is presented in the circumstance that the under-graduate student is not always, perhaps not usually, a member of an institution of learning entirely of his own voluntary choice; but that he has become such in compliance with the wishes of his parents and friends; often with no other feeling on his own part than a desire to make his college life pass away as agreeably as circumstances will allow; a desire which does not always prompt him to seek for enjoyment by the most rational means. As the avowed end, however, of the sub-graduate course is mental discipline, the institution would not be true to this end if it failed to make study a necessity; and to hold every student, so far as its means of coercion extend, to the continuous, steady, and faithful performance of his scholastic tasks.

It is this circumstance, principally, which shapes the visible system of instruction in operation in most educational institutions. Since the student is to be held to regular daily effort, it follows that in the absence of a disposition to labor voluntarily sufficiently prevalent to be safely relied on, some effectual means must be employed of verifying the degree of fidelity with which the constantly recurring tasks are performed. Hence is apparent the propriety of requiring the student, at stated and frequently recurring intervals, to show how far he has acquainted himself with the subjects which have been assigned him for study, and how far he has comprehended the explanations and direct instructions which his teacher may have given him on the same subjects. This he can only do, or can best do, by expressing his knowledge in words—that is to say, by recitation. Accordingly, it is primarily for the sake of securing this end, that the recitation system exists, not only in colleges, but in schools generally. According to Sir William Hamilton, all instruction was originally given in the Universities of England, as it continues to be in the continental Universities, by lecture. The colleges and halls which now monopolize the principal work of teaching in those venerable institutions, were erected to provide for the physical wants of the students, and to secure a vigilant supervision over their morals. The officers, called tutors, employed by the colleges for the latter purpose, gradually took upon themselves the character of instructors, by exacting from the youth under their charge a repetition of what they had learned in the public lecture-halls. To this kind of recitation they subsequently added recitation from books. The evident design of the exercise in its origin, was that in which we find its chief utility at present—to insure the attention of the pupil to the subject which he is required to know. The distinctive name given by the French to the officer whose duty it is merely to hear recitations makes it sufficiently evident what idea is associated with the exercise by them. This name—*répétiteur*—suggests to the mind the bare repetition of a task, as that which it is the business of the officer to secure.

Now, the great importance—the indispensable necessity, in fact—of a recitation system as a part, and a principle part, of the plan of operations of an institution designed to secure the mental training of the young, at a period when they can have attained no adequate notion of the value of this discipline, when fondness for amusement is a predominant trait of the character and when the love of learning exists, at best, but as an unsteady and wavering flame, has apparently led to the formation, not only in the popular mind, but even in the judgment of philosophic thinkers, of a notion regarding the position of this exercise among educational appliances, both as to its dignity of function, and as to its own inherent utility, which greatly exaggerates its importance. However general may be the surprise, or however wide the dissent, which this remark may be fated to encounter, it may be pardoned to the undersigned to have made it, since it can lead to no practical difference between him and those whose views may fail to harmonize with his; inasmuch as he has acknowledged the conviction that, to the under-graduate course of instruction, the system of recitation, or of daily examination, is absolutely indispensable; and inasmuch as he is equally free to admit that, if employed at all, its uninterrupted and rigorous prosecution is a condition in the highest degree essential to its utility.

But recitation—repetition—*per se*, is manifestly an exercise which, to the student who is really in earnest in the pursuit of knowledge, is hardly worth the time it occupies. It is not denied that it is an advantage to any man, young or old, to express his ideas on any subject in a definite form of words, nor even that the immature mind is greatly benefited by the effort necessary to do so. All that Melanchthon has said, all that Hamilton has said, all that any panegyrist of the system of daily examination as a means of instruction has said, in regard to the incidental advantages growing out of the method, is admitted without any hesitation. It stimulates emulation, it cultivates self-possession, it encourages or enforces precision of speech, it abates conceit, it convinces of deficiency. But all these resultant benefits presume the immaturity of the learner; and most of them presume furthermore that an unceasing constraint is necessary to compel him to profit by the instructions he receives. The undersigned is nevertheless, fully persuaded that, for minds which have been subjected to such a system of training as our undergraduate course provides, which are to a certain extent already informed, and which are animated to effort by a sincere and earnest desire for higher attainments, no such system of constraint is necessary; and that the plan of daily examination, in so far as it is designed to exert a constraining power over minds like these, is unnecessary and out of place.

In order to be perfectly candid, however, the admissions already made will be even still further extended. It will be conceded that, considered as an instructive and not as a coercive method, the system of daily examination is attended with some incidental advantages besides those which have just been enumerated. It is a possibility that a student who has failed to comprehend some point embraced in the text of his lesson, may be enlightened by listening to the performance of a fellow-student. It is also a possibility, or rather a fact of frequent occurrence, that the imperfect performance of an individual scholar, may indicate to the instructor the deficiencies of that individual, and so elicit explanatory comments or illustrations. It is further true that the instructor may volunteer explanations and elucidations of points of difficulty, even though occasion may not arise to force their introduction. An acute instructor, moreover, by the ingenious selection of interrogatories, will bring out the weak points of a pupil, as a lawyer does those of a witness; or will bring into prominent relief the points of the subjects under consideration which are of highest importance. But beyond this, it is certainly true that it is only in so far as, for whatever reason, the instructor does actually superadd his own teachings to the text of the lesson, that any talents or attainments which may belong to him personally can be of any sort of use to his pupils. For all the purposes of *mere* recitation, any man who is capable of understanding what the pupil says, and of reading the book or books from which he has learned it, so as to compare the performance with the text, is as good and as capable a presiding officer and examiner in a class-room, as any other. The teacher, therefore, who meets his classes for no purpose at any time but to "hear their recitations," is not really a teacher, except in so far as he engrafts upon this exercise the expository feature which is the distinguishing characteristic of the plan of instruction by lecture. To do this, however, to any extent, in the recitation-room, without seriously interfering with the specific design for which the exercise of recitation was primarily instituted, is proved by experience to be impracticable. Class recitations have, at best, the great disadvantage, that either but few out of a large number can perform at all, or that each one who performs shall be under examination for so brief a space of time as nearly to defeat every useful object, and to render the exercise little better than an idle form.

And here we have the key to one of the causes which divest the exercise of daily examination of much of its assumed value. In a class, or a division of a class, of forty students—and this number is not an unusual one—if each individual is called upon to perform in a recitation of an hour's duration, each will have, as the time in which to display his proficiency—no allowance being made for moments lost in passing from one to another, in pointing out passages in the classics, in enunciating the data of problems in the mathematics, and in other similar ways—exactly one minute and a half. Give each one who performs five minutes (which is certainly not a large allowance), and not one third of the class can be taken up at each exercise. These facts the student can observe, these calculations the student can make, as well as the teacher; and it follows as a necessary consequence, that the recitation system, considered as a system of *coercion*, largely fails of its object; while in regard to the points in which there is claimed for it an *educational* efficiency, its usefulness is correspondingly reduced.

Another serious vice of the system is its pernicious influence on the teacher. To whatever degree it may be coercive to the student, it is not in the least so to him. It stimulates him to no self-improvement, and awakens in him no ambition for higher attainments, on the one hand; and it affords him no adequate field for the display of genius, or for the turning of accumulated knowledge to use, on the other. Instead of this, the opportunity which it offers him of sinking, without observation, into a mere cypher, is a real, a perpetual, and a most insidious temptation to sloth. The difficulty of employing, in the recitation-room, the expository mode of instruction, without encroaching too far upon the exercise proper to the hour, is enough in itself to repress in the teacher the teaching spirit, and to cause him constantly to tend to the level of the mere *répétiteur*. How dangerously is this tendency increased, by the fact that its downward direction coincides precisely with that in which the native love of ease is perpetually dragging all mankind! For this great evil there is but one antagonistic influence which can be of any avail: it is that of a living, fervent, zeal in his work, existing in the instructor himself; a zeal, not in the work of conducting recitations, as the remark might seem to imply, but which would be ridiculous,—a zeal rather in the higher and nobler work of training immortal minds to vigor, and capacitating them for usefulness. The college officer, therefore, of the present day, whose interest in his profession is bounded by the fact, certainly uninspiring, however important to himself, that it secures to him the means of living, is in imminent danger of lapsing into a mere automaton.

The drift of the foregoing observations will now be perceived. In the higher department of the University, it is proposed to employ the plan of recitation only to a limited extent; and in so far as this plan is recommended at all, it is not that it may serve as a coercive power impelling the student to diligence, but rather that the instructor himself may be enabled by its aid to discover in what direction his efforts are most needed. This he may do, either by recitations held at stated times regularly recurring, or by similar exercises appointed at his own discretion, as he may consider them to be needed.

The proposition is, however, to give instruction in this department mainly by oral exposition on the part of the teacher. According to this plan, if the teacher possesses any knowledge on the subject of study which is not contained in the books of the course, or not easily accessible to the student, or if the sources from which such knowledge may be obtained are above the present level of the student's capacity, this knowledge will be brought out and made available. And if he possesses any power of clear analysis, of luminous illustration; if he possesses, as he ought, in order to occupy fitly a position of this high responsibility, that mastery over his theme which belongs to the man who has ceased to think of the truth which he teaches as of a something found in books, and of which all that he knows is knowledge gathered at second-hand; but who has independently interrogated the sources of information himself, and stands in immediate contact with nature and with thought, feeling no need of an interpreter,—if this is his own intellectual character, this the degree of his intellectual cultivation, and this the comprehensive scope of his acquired resources,—then his teachings will carry with them to the minds of his hearers a fulness of satisfaction, and fasten themselves there with a permanency of impression such as no amount of perusal of mere lifeless text-books, written down to the level of their immediate attainments, no matter how earnestly attentive, or how conscientiously faithful the perusal may be, can ever produce.

Not that from such a system of instruction, books are to be discarded. By no means. Not only will the necessity of books continue to be as absolutely imperative as under any system whatever of recitation from a text; but the multiplication of books will be an inevitable consequence. For while the instructor will aim to expound all that relates to theory or doctrine, he will not embarrass his class-room with the lumber of innumerable applications, which, however useful they may be, are the proper labor of the student himself in his solitary study; neither, in regard to simple matters of plain fact, of which a multitude are strewn along the path of every walk in science, will he consider it expedient to occupy time in stating in minute detail what can be found in every book, and what needs but to be read once to be understood. For their necessary enlightenment in matters such as these, he will refer his pupils to certain selected authors, of which he will designate the portions which require their attention with as much regularity as if they were to be subjected to examination upon the same passages. But he will not always confine himself to one author, nor always give the same author preference; for his business is to teach a subject and not a book; and books, therefore, are not his guides but his helps. Nor will the student find it quite a practicable thing to disregard the recommendations thus made, or to neglect the perusal, or rather severe study, of the books designated; for he will shortly discover that this study is indispensable to his understanding and properly profiting by the instructions of his own immediate teacher.

The two salient merits of the method of instruction here proposed, then, for the class of learners contemplated, are first, that it both permits and compels the teacher to *be* a teacher; and neither constrains nor allows him to sink into inactivity, nor to content himself with presiding in empty state over an exercise to which he is conscious of contributing nothing valuable:

and secondly, that it makes *knowledge itself*, and not the substance of any *treatise* upon knowledge, not any *artificial form* into which knowledge has been thrown, the immediate subject of teaching.

In the actual execution of the plan in this University, it is proposed to introduce a feature somewhat peculiar, which appears to be well adapted to increase its usefulness. This is to afford to the members of the class pursuing their studies in any school, the opportunity, after the instructor shall have completed the exposition of the topic of the day, to bring up for re-examination points which still remain to them obscure, or to ask further information in regard to matters which may not have been fully explained. This is, in fact, to inaugurate a species of recitation in which the student and teacher reverse the positions usual in this exercise. The student questions; the teacher replies. The student should even be permitted, if he pleases, in cases which admit of argument, to take issue with his instructor, and to present his reasons for his opinions. Discussion will be advantageous to both parties, and will keep more actively alive the interest felt by the class in the subject of study. It is hardly necessary to add that, by the encouragement of the usages here recommended, it is not intended in any manner to countenance the introduction of trivial or frivolous questions; but on the other hand, supposing the practice to be carried out with a sincere desire on the part of the learner to profit, and on the part of the instructor to bestow benefit, it is one of which the possible utility is too obvious to require to be enforced by argument.

Nothing has thus far been said in regard to the duration proper to be given to the successive courses of sub-graduate and post-graduate study. That is a subject which may perhaps with propriety be left for the independent consideration and determination of the Board of Trustees. Columbia College, New York, under its new organization, proposes to confer the degree of Bachelor of Arts at the end of three years of study; and that of Master of Arts, after two years additional. Brown University has fixed the course for the degree of Bachelor of Philosophy at three years; while that for Bachelor of Arts is suffered still to extend to four years. In the University of Virginia, degrees are conferred only on proficiency, whatever be the time of study necessary to secure the necessary qualification; but in that institution, it is believed that a faithful student can attain the Bachelor's degree in three years, and the Master's in four or five. Whatever be the lengths of time fixed on as proper for the case of this University, it is clearly expedient that here, as at the University of Virginia, proficiency and not a determinate period of residence, should be made the test of fitness for the honor of graduation; and that the degree of proficiency of candidates should not be a mere matter of inference from the recorded results of their daily performances,—a criterion fallacious in the extreme,—but should be directly ascertained at the close of the course, by rigid written examinations.

Were the University of Mississippi an institution having no higher a duty to discharge than that which is immediately visible, and no higher destiny to fulfil than that which she is fulfilling to-day, the undersigned might at this point feel at liberty to lay down his pen. But with a deep conviction pressing upon his mind that this is not the case, he feels irresistibly impelled to trespass still further upon your attention.

The considerations already presented are believed, indeed, to be sufficient in themselves to show the expediency of the change which it is the object of this communication to propose. The oppressiveness of the existing system, the fallacious promise which it holds out to the learner and the public, of thorough instruction in twenty subjects within a time scarcely adequate to the proper mastery of one, and the degree to which these things impair the efficiency of the system itself for the purposes contemplated in its theory, but which in practice, have been almost left out of sight, constitute an overwhelming mass of argument in favor of a measure doubly recommended, at the same time, by its fitness at once to afford relief and to secure a higher order of mental culture. But while these anticipated benefits *are* thus sufficient to justify and even to demand the adoption of the measure recommended, and while therefore the advisability of the measure is placed distinctly upon the basis of its own independent merits, the undersigned does not hesitate candidly to avow that the change proposed is a project especially favorite with him, and that its inauguration, should it receive your sanction, will be regarded by him with especial satisfaction, for a reason entirely distinct from the former—the consideration that the University, in conforming itself to the new plan of organization, will take a first decided step in the direction of that higher development toward which its relations to the general educational system of the State, and its peculiarly responsible position in reference to the State itself—not only as the nursery of the unfolding intellect of her sons, but as the most prominent representative of her intellectual character and the most significant index of her grade in the world of letters and science—bind it continually to look; and toward which all who are in any manner, directly or remotely, connected with its management, its Faculty, its Board of Trustees, the Legislature of the State, and the people of the State themselves, ought constantly, by every stimulating influence at their command, to impel it to advance. In every act of legislation affecting the operations of an institution destined, like this, to exert forever an influence incalculably vast over all the future of a great and powerful people, destined at some coming and not very distant period to do more than any other single cause—nay more than all other single causes combined—to stamp upon the intellectual character of Mississippi the impress it is to wear, to determine the respectability of the State in the eyes of mankind, to stimulate her industry, to multiply the sources of her material wealth, to elevate and purify the tastes of her people, to enlarge their capacities for happiness, and to enable them to fill up those capacities by supplying them with continually growing means of rational enjoyment—in every act affecting the operations of such an institution, it is not merely the exigencies of the *present* which are to be regarded; but it is that grave and weighty mission whose responsibilities extend far forward into the future, and whose influences are to be felt so long as the State of Mississippi shall have a place upon the map of the world—*this* it is above all things which is to enter into and give its color to the decision of every important question which the governing body is called on to decide.

Nor let it be said that the magnitude or the permanence of the influence thus prospectively ascribed to the University is exaggerated. The University is to be the prime mover of the entire educational system of the State. The character of every school, from the highest to the lowest, within our borders, is to be determined ultimately by the respectability or the inferiority of this. Though it is true that but a fraction of the people will receive their personal instruction within the University halls, yet all, without exception, will be partakers of the benefits of which the University is to be the fountain-head and the central source. If the institution does not immediately teach the entire people, it will teach their teachers; or; what is equivalent to this, it will force every instructor whom it does not itself instruct, to come up to the standard it prescribes, on penalty of being else driven from the educational field.

Thus the University is destined in coming time to act, invisibly it may be sometimes, but always powerfully, in every county, and district, and neighborhood in the State; even as already in its infancy, its influence is beginning, in one quarter and another, to be perceptibly marked, elevating the character and improving the efficiency of all other schools. For this influence cannot be confined within limits, nor restricted to any particular grade of educational agency. It will comprehend no less those common schools, in which the children of all the people receive the first elements of their instruction, than those more pretending seminaries in which science and classical learning are placed within the reach of the aspiring student; or the colleges which professedly plant themselves upon its own level. This immense, and in the inevitable tendencies of things, hereafter to become all-controlling, power over the whole educational system of a populous State, imparting its tone and color to the instruction given in every town, and village, and neighborhood, and household, is one of the possession of which the University cannot divest itself if it would, and in regard to the exercises of which it cannot be permitted to choose or to refuse. As the honorable preeminence which it implies has been neither usurped nor arrogated, so the responsibilities which it involves can neither be declined or shaken off. With a conviction of this important truth, every member of the enlightened body of Trustees which at present presides over its interests and controls its destinies, is believed to be deeply penetrated. And whenever any important measure is originated within that body itself, or is proposed to the same body from without, of which the effect may be to modify permanently the modes in which the University discharges its functions, it is believed that a no less inquiring and anxious attention will be given to the consequences which the proposed innovation may entail for good or for ill upon that distant future which the action or non-action of to-day must affect, than to the advantages or disadvantages which may promise to be its immediate results.

Therefore it is that the undersigned feels it to be a duty, to insist strongly upon the view that the measure proposed herein for the deliberation of the Board is one which is demanded in order to the just fulfilment of that high responsibility which rests upon the University, in consequence of its peculiar relations to the educational system of the State. The institution would be faithless to its trust, if its tendencies were not always upward. The hour has arrived in which it is proper and fitting that it should take, so far as its visible arrangements and instrumentalities are concerned, the first upward step. That it has been, internally and inconspicuously to the public eye, heretofore steadily advancing in improvement from year to year, is at least to be hoped and is certainly believed. The time has come when, ceasing to be content with improving what it is, it shall cultivate the nobler ambition which aims actually to be something more than it is—something more comprehensive in its scope—something more far-reaching in its purposes. Not that it should abandon the ground it at present occupies, or cease to discharge its present functions. The position which it actually holds it should still maintain substantially unaltered; and the system of instruction in operation within its walls to-day, should still be preserved unchanged, except in what concerns its more energetic prosecution, and its improved efficiency.

But what *is* the University of to-day? What but a training school for immature minds—impaired, indeed, in its usefulness for this purpose by the very attempt to accomplish, along with it, other and entirely incompatible objects? If the people suppose that this is a place to make practical men, or learned men, or profoundly scientific men—if they suppose that it is within the reach of possibility for the University, under the existing system, to turn out accomplished engineers, or expert chemists, or proficient astronomers, or profound philosophers, or even finished scholars—we know very well that they are deceived. Not that this institution falls any farther short of accomplishing these ends, or fails any more signally to meet this popular impression, than other American colleges; but that the power to do these things seems, by force of a general hallucination, to be attributed to colleges as a class, while, in point of fact, it does not actually exist in any one of the whole number. At least, if any exception is to be made from this remark, it can only be of those which have already introduced into their plan of organization, some modification substantially like that which it is proposed to-day to introduce into the University of Mississippi.

This University is, then, at this time but a school for youth of minds still immature. What this class of learners require is mental discipline, mental culture, mental development,—not the obtrusion of a flood of information, no matter how valuable, in regard to every subject of human knowledge, upon minds unprepared to receive it, or to store it systematically away, or to turn it to the uses to which it is capable of being applied. Why should we not, while engaged in this great preliminary work of education, adopt the only course which is truly efficient, that of confining to it our entire and exclusive attention. If education has really two great and broadly distinguished functions to fulfil —to operate on the mind itself, and to furnish it with material for its own future operations—to draw out or *educe* its faculties, and to supply the same faculties with the aliment which is to maintain their subsequent vigor —and if nature herself points out the order in which these functions should succeed each other, why should we disregard her obvious indications, or neglect to conform our practice as well to the dictates of common sense as to the principles of a sound philosophy? If we admit the justice of this reasoning, why should we hesitate to draw a distinct line of division between the period devoted to the first great educational end, and that allotted to the second? Even should we propose to ourselves to do no more than we have hitherto done in behalf of positive learning or positive science, can any good reason be assigned why we should scruple to say, it is here that the first of our labors ceases, and here that the second begins? No reason at all, good or otherwise, for not doing this, can exist, unless it be that the moment we make such an avowal, we shall feel ourselves bound to enter upon the second part of our task with the purpose, with the arrangements, and with the instrumentalities, which shall render its results, what they are far enough from being now, a substantial reality. We shall feel ourselves bound, in short, to rise above the grade of the German gymnasium—which is precisely our grade of to-day—and to assume, by approaches which the force of circumstances may indeed make gradual, but which must be no less steady and persevering, the character of the German university.

But this is precisely the thing which, in the view of the undersigned, it is our manifest duty to do. It is not every college, indeed, upon which such an obligation rests, any more than it would be the duty of every gymnasium in Germany to aspire to transform itself into a university. It is by no means necessary that the schools for what is called supplementary education—

schools which open up to all comers the way to the most thorough attainments in each special department of letters and science—should be as numerous as the colleges. And even if it were so, it is manifestly impossible that the colleges of this country should become generally universities. In order that an institution of the highest learning may exist at all, the first of all necessities is an ample endowment. There is not a college in the whole country which can provide itself with books, and instruments, and collections in natural science, and all the other appliances essential to thorough instruction, with no resources beyond the fees paid in by students for their tuition. There is not one which can even pay its officers for their services, unless it be upon a scale which starves rather than compensates, if it possess no better reliance than this. The higher education in this country, in the words of Dr. Wayland, is the cheapest of all commodities in the market. It is thrown, in fact, into the market so far below its cost, that it may, with all but literal truth, be said to be given away. There is nothing in this, indeed, to be regretted, so long as the quality of the education thus furnished is not vitiated by its cheapness. There would be nothing to be regretted, if it were not only almost, but absolutely and altogether given away. For this would be only for a community to supply one of its own indispensable necessities after the cheapest manner. Neither would the wealth apparently consumed in the operation be by any means sunk or lost. The process is simply a transfer of a given value from the benefactor—the college corporation or the State—to the beneficiary, who is the student; and the value transferred is at the same time transformed into a more useful shape: from inert it is converted into living gold. Among all the investments which it ever entered into the heart of the most greedy capitalist to conceive, there is none so productive as this. Nature only has provided any thing like it, in the case in which she returns, for the seed committed to her bosom, some an hundred fold, some sixty, and some thirty.

There would be nothing to be regretted, if not only the higher education, but if all education, in all its grades, were given away; by which, of course, nothing can be meant but that it should be furnished to all the people at the expense of all the people. For this would only be to alter the mode of making an investment, which ought, as no sensible man will pretend to deny, by all means to be made. The people ought to be educated; and by whatever system this is done, the people must ultimately pay for their own education. They pay at present irregularly, unsystematically, and unequally; and the thing is done ill. They might pay according to some just and equal rule; and then, all education, from the highest to the lowest, being controlled by the State itself, and subjected to one uniform, consistent, and enlightened method, it would be done well, and the same opportunities would be extended equally to every citizen.

But this matter is aside from the purpose of the

present communication. It will be observed that the undersigned regards the cheapness of the higher education as a gratifying circumstance, only with the reserve of an important proviso, that the quality of the education thus furnished shall not be vitiated by its cheapness.

It is much to be apprehended, however, that the prejudicial consequence here hinted at, is too often a reality. If it is true that, in the present stage of the world's advancement, science cannot be properly taught without costly apparatus; if it is true, also, that without opportunity of access to many books, without, in other words, expensive libraries, the learning of instructors cannot be profound; if it is still further true that, in the educational field, as in every other, high attainments and brilliant talents cannot be commanded unless they are adequately compensated,—then it is self-evidently manifest that colleges of humble endowments, or of no endowments at all, cannot furnish to their students educational advantages equal to those offered by institutions in this respect more favored. Without, however, for the moment insisting upon this point, it is safe at least to say that such colleges can never rise to the rank of universities; and it may be added that it is not desirable that they should.

It is nevertheless a fact that true universities are at this moment among the most urgent of the intellectual wants of our country. And it is an important circumstance that there is already in existence a class of collegiate institutions whose relations to the municipal authorities of the States within which they exist point them out as the agencies most fit to supply this want. In addition to this, the resources of these institutions are also, in some instances at least, already adequate to the demand which the imposition upon them of this higher function would create. This is especially the case with the University of Mississippi, the accumulated proceeds of whose original munificent endowment by the Congress of the United States, were stated by Gov. McRae, in a message to the Legislature two years ago, at more than one million of dollars. Of this fund, the Legislature, in the original act of charter creating the University, committed to your honorable body the exclusive control. And though, by a subsequent act of legislation, this provision of the charter was repealed, and the Legislature resumed to itself the control over the trust, yet, whenever the necessities of the University have required appropriations, such appropriations have always been cheerfully granted, and they may with reasonable confidence be equally relied on for the future.

The University, then, is amply provided with the resources necessary to enable it satisfactorily to discharge those high responsibilities which have been pointed out as properly resting upon it. For its present operations, its immediate income is sufficient. It is only necessary that the law of 1856 be permanently extended—and this must be done, in any event, if the Legislature would not thrust down the institution below its present level instead of permitting it to rise—and it is hardly probable that further drafts upon the fund will be needed within the lifetime of the present generation. For the generations which are to succeed, we may safely trust to the enlightened intelligence of the Legislatures into whose hands the guardianship of this inestimably important trust shall then devolve.

From what has been said, the inference follows that the State universities of the Union occupy the position and possess generally the resources which make it both fit and practicable for them to supply the great educational want which has just been signalized. Some of them, among which the University of Michigan deserves honorable mention, have from the beginning recognized their obligation in this respect; and without discarding, or in any important particular modifying, the collegiate feature common to all institutions of the same grade, have organized themselves under the visible form of true universities.

Thus far in this argument, the want of institutions of a higher than merely collegiate grade has been assumed and asserted as an unquestionable fact. The assertion may not, nevertheless, be suffered to pass without question; and accordingly there can be no impropriety in looking for a moment into the evidence on which it rests. Now, the existence of the want as a reality is made evident by the earnest and urgent demand, spoken of earlier in this communication, which has been, for the last thirty or forty years, so extensively heard, for something or other which the existing educational system does not supply. This demand, so far as it has proceeded from scholars and men of science, has taken the specific form of a demand for universities called by that name; because scholars and men of science have been able to perceive distinctly that the university was the precise thing needed to satisfy the want. But when it has come from the people—and from the people it has come very steadily for at least a quarter of a century—it has been, not for the university by name, but for new schools of some vaguely conceived description; for colleges to be broken up and destroyed in all that regards the province of their past usefulness, and built up anew upon some visionary plan and according to some impracticable theory; for schools of science as applied to the arts of construction, of agriculture, of manufactures and every thing useful to mankind, but chiefly things useful according to that literal sense which confounds utility with increase of wealth; for schools, in short, which should do what the collegiate schools do not do, and what we know that it is not necessary or even proper that they should do—prepare men, so far as schools can prepare them, to take directly hold of the real business of life. No one is ignorant that this demand has existed for a period at least as long as asserted; that at times it has been vociferous and violent; or that, not content with insisting on the creation of new schools to accomplish the ends desired, it has turned occasionally, almost in a spirit of vindictive destructiveness, upon the old, because they did not accomplish those same ends.

These demands, the undersigned ventures to assert, are evidence of the want of higher universities. Not because they ask for the university; not because their authors, if the university were proposed to them as a remedy, would be likely to accept it; but because the present inconvenience which is so sensibly felt, is one which the university would remove, though those who feel it do not perceive how. And why not? Because first, looking at universities as they have been in past centuries, as the repositories of literary lore, as the resorts of scholars dealing with abstractions, as the burrowing places of bookworms eating out the hearts of the black-letter volumes of the sixteenth century or of the manuscripts of the sixth, as the unchallenged domain of grammarians and lexicographers, of commentators upon Aristotle and Longinus, ingenious speculators upon the mysteries of the digamma, and indefatigable elaborators of ethical and logical niceties, they picture them in their imaginations, even to this hour, as solemn and shadowy retreats, still smelling of the dust and mould of antiquity, where philology, linguistic philosophy, and the sublimer metaphysics brood, like the pensive owl in Gray's churchyard turret, with none to

> "Molest their ancient solitary reign."

But this conception is entirely erroneous. The University, in the sense in which the name is now generally received, no matter what may have been its original acceptation, is *Universitas Scientiarum;* it is, in other words, an institution in which the highest learning of its day is taught in every walk of human knowledge. When classical learning, philosophy, and logic, were subjects of the highest interest in human estimation, it is not surprising that the character of university teaching should have been principally determined by them. But inasmuch as, at the present day, physical science has attained a position of actual dignity immeasurably higher than it then enjoyed, and as its useful applications have become almost endlessly more numerous and varied, the university of to-day would fail to be what its name imports, if it did not assign a corresponding prominence to these subjects,—subjects, be it observed, which happen to be the same for which the agitators we have been speaking of demand that a special provision of special schools shall be made.

There is, however, a second class of agitators, who, while admitting the justice of the foregoing representation, are not disposed to accept the university as a remedy for the inconvenience which they suffer, because, while it gives them all that they demand, it gives them at the same time much more—much for which they do not ask, and for which they do not care. They fear so great a project as the creation of an institution professing and really preparing itself to teach every thing embraced in the entire circle of human knowledge. They fear that, in attempting this, they shall attempt what is beyond their means; and that by grasping too much, they shall lose every thing. It is believed that all this class of persons, if they rightly interpret our views, will find that we are entirely in accordance with them, and they with us. For no such visionary scheme is entertained by any one connected with this institution, as that of creating here in a day, a university complete in all the many-faced aspects of a repository of universal truth, and a dispenser of universal knowledge. What is aimed at, what is recommended, is only, as already stated, to take a first step in the right direction—a step which shall, indeed, ultimately conduct to the fulfilment of the great idea, but which shall not be itself the fulfilment—a step which will mark only the beginning of a progress, in which advancing only as the growing intelligence and increasing wants of the people of the State shall urge it, the University of Mississippi may, to the eyes of a future generation, at length present the lustrous spectacle which the comprehensive idea of a true university implies.

There is, however, still another class of persons, whose views on this subject ought not to be overlooked, though they are a class who do not agitate—a class who, on the other hand, are well enough satisfied with things as they are, and whose quiet contentment results from the belief that the age has no wants which the colleges do not or cannot supply. This class of men fully admit all that is said of the value of modern science; but then they suppose that no better schools of science than the colleges are needed. Taking up the prospectus of the college course of study and receiving it as true to the letter, it is not surprising that they are led into error. They observe this prospectus to embrace the titles of all the sciences whose usefulness is most extolled, to say nothing of many others, such as zoology, botany, and the remaining branches of natural history, concerning the usefulness of which their notions are less clear; and resting on the largeness of the promise, which they accept as evidence of performance, they turn round and demand the use of making any new provision for that which, according to the showing of more than a hundred official publications, is abundantly provided for already. It is believed that the number of those who thus plant themselves as obstructions in the way of the improvement of higher education in America, is not small. It is believed that there are even some such in our own State, looking on with jealous eyes, while propositions are in agitation which involve a higher development within the University of Mississippi. Why should there not be multitudes of this description everywhere, when it is considered that more than a hundred thousand of the fallacious promises of colleges in regard to this matter are annually sown broadcast over the whole land! Let such persons be only correctly informed—let them take the simple exhibit presented in the earlier pages of this letter as their guide—and, assuredly, respecting science, and honoring science, and feeling as they do the need of a more general diffusion of a science which is sound and solid, instead of being unsubstantial and shadowy, they must, if it were

4

only to preserve their own consistency, go along with those whom they now regard as idle innovators.

There is still another class whose views on the subject under consideration cannot be overlooked—a class possibly the most numerous of all those who concern themselves about it; or, if not the most numerous, at any rate, by far the most impracticable. Those are here indicated who deny the utility of high learning altogether. They are, of course, utilitarians in the technical sense of that word. Let any thing tend to promote the bodily comfort of the race—let it furnish man with food, or keep him warm, or put a barrier between him and the weather—and that is a useful thing. By consequence, therefore, science does, occasionally, in some of its practical results, command their partial consideration; but for science or learning as a whole, a matter between which and the increase of wealth no connection in the relation of cause and effect is to their minds obvious, they have no respect whatever. To elevate the intellectual man in the scale of being, to enable him to form larger and juster views than his unaided senses or his individual, casual, and unsystematic observation has qualified him to conceive, of the power and wisdom and goodness of the great Architect of the universe, to introduce him to a world of enjoyments growing out of the exercise of the godlike intellect upon subjects of beauty, and sublimity, and deep-seated and with delightfully difficult effort laboriously unraveled truth,—enjoyments such as doubtless occupy cherubic intelligences in their rapt contemplation of the wonderful works of God,—all this the mere utilitarian philosopher, ever like the man with the muck-rake in Bunyan, looking downward, fails to comprehend and to appreciate; and all arguments addressed to him, founded upon the consideration, to which he is insensible, that knowledge is valuable for its own sake, are wholly thrown away.

And yet, is there not a dignity in knowledge? And is not intellectual wealth a priceless treasure, even though it be that kind of intellectual wealth which heaps no delicacies ravished from tropical climes upon the board of the banqueter, and clothes no luxurious limbs with the spoil of the gorgeous East? If this be not true, then God certainly has made man in vain. The domestic animals, which spend their contented lives in his society; the dog, for instance, which wastes his idle days untasked by any toil save the light labor of the chase, or such other trivial services as his instincts prompt him to enjoy, if he be but comfortably housed, and sufficiently fed, and kindly treated by his master,—is happy, quite as happy as a dog can be. And the human animal, who cultivates only his lower propensities, or at best, of his mental powers allows only the humbler to be active, though he may be somewhat more discriminating than the brute in regard to the degrees of luxurious enjoyment, yet he too, when he is warmed and filled and handsomely sheltered, he too is happy; but he is no happier than the dog. Surely we were born for something nobler than this! Surely it is a better and a higher happiness which fills up the capacities of our superior nature, when developed by mental discipline, purified by moral culture, and led to look through nature up to nature's God, it expands to the sublime stature of that glorious image in which man was originally created sinless, and makes the fallen mortal to appear, even yet, but a little lower than the angels.

But, abandoning this line of argument, which, however just, has been experimentally found to be practically useless, it is by no means difficult to meet the utilitarian upon his own ground. Or rather, it *is* difficult; and the difficulty springs not out of the lack of material for argument, but out of the embarrassment which attends any attempt at argument at all, upon a subject with which the contending parties are not equally familiar; and in some degree also out of the invariable propensity of the objector in this case to raise up trivial side-issues, and to resort to idle special pleading.

If, in what follows, the undersigned has chosen to confine himself chiefly or entirely to subjects connected with physical science, this is only because in the measures projected for the improvement of the University, it is science chiefly which involves the question of expense.

Is, then, scientific knowledge useful? Few objectors will take the broad ground of denying all utility to science; or of denying utility to all sciences. Few will hesitate to admit that every science furnishes some facts that are useful. Even the patient and diligent collector of bugs, and butterflies, and caterpillars, though looked down upon in a general way by the utilitarian with an amusingly sublime loftiness of contemptuous regard, if he but intimate a belief that he is upon the sure trace of a method of exterminating the insect scourges of the cotton-field, is listened to with respectful, nay, with greedy ears, and is elevated at once to a position of comparative dignity. No scoffer at science, therefore, ever scoffs at the science, or at the facts of science, which he understands; understands, that is to say, not as simple, isolated facts, a thing which is generally easy,—but understands in all their bearings and relations, and far-reaching affiliations with other facts with which they have no obvious or visible connection—a thing which is often not easy at all. And it is because of this difficulty, because many of the most valuable of all the facts which science has revealed, present themselves to the general mind with no evidence of their usefulness about them,—hence it is that the objectors, abandoning every position which permits to meet them upon the basis of their own knowledge, resort to that vexatious system of special pleading to which allusion has been made, and demand that we shall demonstrate the utility of detached truths, one after another in endlessly provoking detail, which they do *not* understand. The case is even worse than this. In every branch of human investigation some truths may possibly be brought to light which are merely incidental to the inquiry, and are without perceptible ulterior importance: precisely as in working a quarry, some fragments of granite or marble may be encountered which are well enough as fragments of a mountain, but which are hardly worth the trouble of carting away. Now, though in science it is hardly safe to say that any truth, however seemingly insignificant, may not have, wrapped up within it, a latent value which may yet draw towards it the admiring attention of all mankind; and though experience has shown that it is becoming, every day we live, less and less safe to dogmatize on these subjects, yet it is not to be denied that here and there a solitary fact may, by dint of great diligence, be hunted up, which science has made known and recorded, but of which we may deem it no shame to confess that we know not at this moment how to put it to use. Now, it is precisely upon this unhappy class of facts, of immediately doubtful utility or of no presently known utility at all, that the decriers of scientific research are always ready to descend. And yet it is a matter entirely notorious to every one in the slightest degree acquainted with the history of science, that in the whole list of truths which investigation has revealed, there is hardly a single one which, at the time of its discovery, and in some instances long after, did not stand in this same unfortunate class. The truth is, that speculations upon the value of any discovery whatever, in the moment in which the discovery is made, are totaly idle—are worse than idle—are foolish. The alchemists, in their indefatigable though empirical and blind researches in quest of the philosopher's stone, discovered many curious compounds which, since they availed nothing towards the production of gold, were held by them in low esteem; yet among these are some of those energetic re-agents which, in the hands of modern chemistry, and directed by modern intelligence, have heaped up gold in mountains beyond even the alchemist's wildest dreams, in the heart of every civilized land.

To descend to later times, and to speak with more specific particularity, when Priestly, in 1774, turning the focus of his burning lens upon the substance known in the shops of the apothecaries under the name of red precipitate, detached bubbles of a gas identical with that which, in the atmosphere, supports life, who could presume that, in thus freeing one of the metals from its companion element, he had detected the composition of many of the most useful ores, and furnished a hint which was yet to reduce all metallurgic art, from the smelting of iron to the reduction of aluminum, under the dominion of chemical science, and to the severe rule of an intelligent and a productive economy? When, in the same year, Scheele, by operating on the acid of sea-salt, made first visible to human eyes that beautifully colored gas whose suffocating odor is now so well known to all the world, who could foresee the astonishing revolution which a discovery then interesting only for its curious beauty, was destined to introduce into the manufacture of paper, of linen textures, and of a vast multitude of other objects, of daily and hourly use? Or what imagination could have been extravagant enough or fantastic enough in the exercise of its inventive power, to anticipate that a substance, for the moment not merely useless but seemingly noxious, would in the nineteenth century accomplish what without it, no instrumentality known to science or art could have accomplished,—find aliment for the rapacious maw of a letter-press whose insatiable demands, already grown vast beyond all conception, grow yet with each succeeding year? When the chemists of the last century observed the discoloration and degradation which certain metallic salts undergo in the sunlight, who could possibly read, in a circumstance so apparently trivial though occasionally troublesome, the intimation that the sun himself was about to place in the hands of Niepce, and Daguerre, and Talbot, a pencil whose magical powers of delineation should cause the highest achievements of human pictorial art to seem poor and rude in the comparison? When Malus, in 1810, watching the glare of the sun's rays reflected from the windows of the Luxembourgh to his own, noticed for the first time the curious phenomena attendant on that peculiar condition of light which has since been known by the name of polarization, what prescience could have connected a fact so totally without any perceptible utility, with the manufacture of sugar in France; or have anticipated that an instrument founded in principle on this very property, would, forty years later, effect an annual saving to the French people to the extent of hundreds of thousands of francs? When Œrsted, in 1819, observed the disturbance of the magnetic needle by the influence of a neighboring galvanic current, how wild and visionary would not that man have been pronounced to be, who should have professed to read in an indication so slight, the grand truth that science had that day stretched out the sceptre of her authority over a winged messenger, whose fleetness should make a laggard even of Oberon's familiar sprite, and render the velocity which could "put a girdle round the earth in forty minutes," tardy and unsatisfying?

Questions of this kind, suggested by the history of scientific progress, might be multiplied to fill a volume. Indeed, it has almost come to be a dogma in science, that there is no new truth whatever, no matter how wide a space may seem, in the hour of its discovery, to divide it from any connection with the material interests of man, which carries not within it the latent seeds of a utility, which further discovery in the same field will reveal and cause to germinate. And it has also almost come to be a rule, that new discoveries in regard to the properties of material things, or of the laws that govern them, *shall* belong to the class of seemingly useless truths. For the obvious applications of known natural laws, the obvious utilities inherent in familiar physical qualities, have, under the untiring scrutiny of myriads of penetrating eyes, been long since brought to light, and, inwrought into the endlessly varied operations of human art, have been made tributary to the service of mankind. The superficial placers have all been overrun and exhausted; the golden sands of the pleasant river valleys have yielded up their dazzling and easily won treasures ; the rifled surface presents no longer any thing to recompense the labor of the eager adventurer; but deep in the everlasting rocks, and locked in an adamantine prison, lies yet the precious object of desire; still attainable, but attainable only at the price of a toil that never tires, as the conquest of an energy which difficulties only stimulate, and as the reward of a patience which no discouragements can exhaust.

The analogy between the two cases here presented, that of the miner for material treasures, and the delver after scientific truth, is up to this point complete. But the gold of the miner is still the same gold, whether it be picked up loose-lying from among the sands of the river, or torn with sweat and toil from the bowels of the earth. The deep-lying truths, on the other hand, which the patient and persevering inquirer succeeds in occasionally bringing, one by one, to the surface, resemble in point of value the gold of the mine, not through identity of uses with truths before known, as gold is identical in properties with other gold, but through their adaptation to new uses which still remain to be brought to light. And thus a new truth of this class, though in its bosom may lie buried the germ of a wealth to which all the gold of California would be but as the light dust of the balance, may yet for years occupy in men's estimations no higher a place than that of a fact of curious knowledge; even as the priceless diamond in the cottage of the fisherman of the eastern tale was esteemed capable of being turned to no better account than to serve as a plaything for children. Not even useful truth is useful until it is known to be so, and until it is known how it is to be so. And no matter how numerous and multiform may be the novel facts which the invading armies of science, in their grand march through the regions of the unknown, may sweep together as their spoil, and no matter what infinity of benefit to man may be hidden among the rich booty—all this availeth nothing to the world which it so deeply concerns, until, by patient study and unwearied perseverance, and experiment endlessly varied and feeling its way cautiously in the obscurity, it has been made manifest to what useful ends the results of the conquest may be applied. Thus, when Volta, by piling up bits of metal and moistened card-board, one upon another, succeeded in producing a feeble disturbance of electrical equilibrium, he discovered, as early as the year 1800, a truth pregnant with consequences of incalculable moment to science, and destined to contribute more to human comfort and the wealth of nations, than the discovery of a dozen Californias. Yet several years elapsed before, in the hands of Davy, the wonderful fertility of this great germ-truth even began to be revealed; and still, at this very day, after the lapse of more than half a century, after a long series of illustrious investigators, some of them made chiefly illustrious by their very association with this subject, have added their labors to his,—after the inventive genius of a Hare, and a Wollaston, and a Daniell, and a Grove, and a Bunsen, have been successively employed in exalting the energy of the combinations, and the intelligent sagacity of an Ampere, an Arago, a Henry, a De la Rive, and a Faraday, have been busying themselves with the applications, and opening out to view a brilliant array of resultant truths; when all things in earth and air and sea have yielded to this next to miraculous power the secret of their composition; when the obdurate puzzle of the earth's magnetism has melted away before it; when a net-work of electric wires has annihilated the breadth of continents, and the two mightiest nations of the earth are preparing to stretch out the line which links thought with thought, from shore to shore of the ocean itself,—even now, the progressive development of the great germ-truth is still unchecked, and the world is full of laborers exploring, with unabated zeal, the field first opened to their research by the intelligent observation and appreciative genius of Volta.

If it is difficult, then, for philosophers themselves to judge, in the first moments of discovery, in what precise form, and through what precise practical application, any new truth may become palpably useful to man, how much more so must it be for the multitude who are not philosophers! And if, in the experience of centuries, it has happened, in instances which defy enumeration, that the insignificant truth of to-day has been exalted to a position of the highest dignity to-morrow, how shall we venture to say, of any known fact of science, however it may surpass our present penetration to discover any connection, immediate or remote, between it and the increase of human wealth or comfort, that it is a useless fact, or that the labor which may have been expended in bringing it to light has been thrown away.

The science of astronomy is that which seems, to the view of most men at the present day, to occupy itself more than any other, with laborious trifling. Not that the uses of astronomy in general, are altogether denied. Most persons know that astronomy has something to do, in some way or other, with navigation; and nobody need be told that navigation has something to do with commerce, or commerce with human wealth. But the idea seems to be generally prevalent, that all the service which astronomy can render to navigation has been rendered long ago, and that observers are now idly gazing up into the skies for the gratification of a transcendentally refined curiosity. The fact then, that this science has already done much to promote men's most substantial interests, seems to be esteemed an argument in disproof of the probability or the prospect of its ever doing more. But it is true, notwithstanding, that astronomy is still too far short of the point of perfection, to assign the place of a ship on the ocean within a narrower limit of error than three or four miles.

Now, the importance to an individual navigator of

being able to determine his longitude, is perhaps intelligible enough to need no illustration; but the importance which commercial nations have always attached to the possession of a general method, which should enable all their navigators, at all times and on every ocean, to do the same, may be best understood by considering what governments have done in order to secure such a method. As early as 1598, Philip III., of Spain, offered a reward of one thousand crowns to the person who should solve the problem. The Dutch States shortly after followed with an offer of ten thousand florins. In 1714, the British Parliament proposed the magnificent prize of twenty thousand pounds to any one who should furnish a method by which longitude on the ocean could be ascertained within thirty geographical miles. The same body offered also the lesser reward of fifteen thousand pounds for a method which should be correct within forty miles; and ten thousand, for one true only within sixty. In 1716, France, under the regency of the Duke of Orleans, offered to the same end, a prize of one hundred thousand livres. But no really important results were ever arrived at, until after the establishment of regular astronomical observatories. When, in 1674, St. Pierre, a French competitor for the prize offered by Parliament, presented to the court of Charles II. an astronomical method for the determination of the longitude, no better tables of the heavenly bodies existed than those of Tycho Brahe. The commissioners appointed to examine St. Pierre's claim, applied for advice to Flamsteed, then the most eminent of British astronomers. He replied that the method was valueless, on account of the errors of the tables; and that every astronomical method must be equally so, unless the places of the heavenly bodies should be observed anew. It is said that Charles, on reading this letter, exclaimed impulsively, "But I must have them observed!" and these words from the lips of royalty laid the foundation of the Observatory at Greenwich. That single institution has done more for the increase of the world's wealth, than would have sufficed to support, at their ease, all the astronomers and physicists that ever lived, since the days of Hipparchus; to build and furnish all the observatories the world ever saw; to establish and endow all the universities, colleges, and schools, of every grade, from highest to lowest, throughout the globe; to erect and provide for all the hospitals, alms-houses, and eleemosynary institutions of every kind, in all civilized lands; and to build all the churches and parsonages, as well as defray all other expenses attendant on the support of religion, in every Christian country, from the advent of our blessed Saviour down to the present hour. To make even a conjectural estimate of the true value of its services to mankind, would, from the nature of the case, be impracticable, since the elements which must enter into such an estimate are as numerous as the endlessly varied articles of human consumption. It is even impossible to make a comparative estimate of the value of astronomical agency considered along with

other agencies concerned in promoting the same interests; since all the improvements of art or science which tend to give increased development to commercial enterprise, and all the stimulating influences which incite men to engage or encourage them to continue in commercial pursuits, steal from astronomy at last half their efficacy, by availing themselves of the security which it has provided for the immense aggregate of treasure constantly afloat upon the waves. But without particularly regarding this circumstance, we need not hesitate to assert that the observatories of Europe, beginning with those of Greenwich and Paris in the seventeenth century, have done more in widening the scope of the world's commercial operations, and quickening the energy which has pervaded and filled them everywhere with activity, than all other influences put together—than the temptation to human cupidity offered from all antiquity in the fabled wealth of India, Cathay, and the Islands of Spices—than the intoxication of that delirium with which the world of the sixteenth century ran mad over the metallic treasures of the two Americas—than the resistless allurement held out during the same historic period, to the spirit of wild adventure, by the uncertain riches of the portions of the New World still unexplored, or by the deep mystery which hung over the silent and yet untempted wastes of the great South Sea—than all the powerful stimulus applied by interested governments, in the form of favoring legislation, grants of monopolies, and the investment of trading

companies with exclusive rights and privileges—than all the improvements of naval architecture, increasing the strength, the stability, the capacity, and the speed of sea-going vessels—than all the discoveries in marine geography, disclosing the hidden dangers of the ocean's bed, and the insidious currents of its surface—than all the progress made in studying the laws which govern the winds, as to their direction, their violence, and their fluctuations; or control the storms that from time to time lash the watery waste into fury—than the natural enlargement of the field, from the up-springing and growth to greatness of colonies upon wild and untenanted shores—than the simultaneous enlargement of the material, by the discovery of new articles adapted to the uses of man, or the application of articles of ancient knowledge to new uses—than the enlargement of human wants, through the facility with which the simpler wants of the earlier centuries are supplied in the later—than the enlargement of human wealth itself, which tends ever, through commercial enterprise, to enlarge itself still more—than, finally, the great improvement of the nineteenth century, the invocation of the powerful arm of steam to the propulsion of the mercantile marine, securing a rapidity and a definite duration of transit on the longest voyages, which are next in value to wealth, itself. Yes—it is repeated—superior to all these influences, and to all other influences which may have operated to give expansion to the commercial enterprise of the world, has been, during the last two centuries, the

increasing security with which its magnificent undertakings have been surrounded by the science of Astronomy, and by the patient, weary, long-continued, seldom adequately appreciated, and never adequately paid, labors of the obscure and neglected astronomer. Obscure in life, neglected in life, jostled to the bottom of the heap in the heterogeneous mixture of human society, where the light weights too usually come uppermost; but in death appreciated, in death magnified, in death honored with statues and monuments, in death made the object of panegyric and eulogy! Attentions how empty and idle! Honors how vain and useless! For the astronomer who has written his name upon the starry heavens, needs no human tongue to praise him, no human monuments to perpetuate his memory; he dies no more. The bright companions of his many painful night-watches, when they miss him at his tube, will whisper his name softly to the spirit of his toiling successor; and so it will go down with a starry lustre about it, from one generation to another, till the last patient sentinel in the celestial watch-tower shall suddenly be arrested in his vocation, and in his latest gaze through the field of his protracted labors, shall behold the heavens themselves rolling together like a scroll!

This great benefit conferred by astronomy upon commerce, and through commerce upon the world's wealth, has resulted from the operation of a very simple principle. In whatever human enterprises wealth is set at hazard, the ventures will be greater in proportion as

the hazard is less. It is conceivable that the dangers of the ocean might be so great as to arrest transmarine commerce altogether. It is also conceivable that they might be totally annihilated, so that commerce by sea should be subject to no greater burthens or discouragements than commerce by land. In this latter state of things, the natural causes stimulating enterprise would have free scope, and produce their full and legitimate effect. Between the extremes, commerce would assume every intermediate aspect of vitality and degree of freedom, from vigorous life and total unrestraint on the one hand, down to absolute torpidity and complete inaction on the other. Now, among the Athenians, according to Say, marine insurance bore the extravagant rate of sixty per cent. per annum, or thirty per cent. per voyage on the total value insured. Say supposes this extraordinary fact to be in part attributable to the barbarous habit of the peoples with whom the Athenians traded; a supposition apparently quite gratuitous, since no producing people is hostile to commerce, and no non-producing people is worth trading with. But he attributes it also, with greater justice, to the dangers of navigation; and adds this significant remark: "There was more danger [to the Athenian merchant-sailors] in a voyage from the Piræus to Trapezus, though but three hundred leagues distant, than there is now [1826] in one from L'Orient to China, which is a distance of seven thousand." This statement alone is sufficient to show that the reduction of marine dangers in modern times—a reduction mainly due to astronomy—has been sufficient, ten times over, to stimulate into vigor a struggling trade; and hence that that rich oriental commerce which lived and flourished, and in the hands of the Venetians, and the Portuguese, and the Dutch, poured wealth into Europe, in spite of the difficulties and dangers—greater than those of ocean—of the overland route, in spite of the indefinite perils and perpetual losses of the tedious voyage by the Cape, in spite of the months of time wasted in the transit during which the capital lay a dead investment—the commerce which under all these disadvantages not only continued to live, but which enriched its possessors, must, under the almost boundless development given to it by the favoring circumstances of modern times, have contributed to the world's wealth to an extent which no figures can compute.

The condition of the astronomical tables at the founding of the Royal Observatory was such, that they could not, by any possibility, be made the basis of a method of practical navigation; since the place of a ship as determined by them, might possibly be in error to the enormous extent of nine hundred miles; nor was it in the power of any correction practicable without new and laborious observation, to reduce this limit of error to less than one fourth of its amount, or nearly two hundred miles. On the establishment of observatories, the first and largest steps toward improvement were comparatively rapid and easy; the more recent have, on the contrary, been slow and difficult. It is so with all progress toward the ideal of perfection. The sculptor blocks out his statue with a bold and heavy hand. The rough and massive fragments fall off in showers upon every side; and, in a space incredibly brief, the figure of the image reveals itself dimly, as if it were already a real existence, smothered beneath a rocky incrustation. But when this rigid veil begins to grow thin, and the looker-on almost expects to see the impatient master tear it impulsively away, then it is that the true labor only commences. Then it is that the coarse chisel and the heavy mallet will serve no longer, but with a more delicate implement, and a more cautious hand, and a more anxiously watchful eye, the master sculptor detaches the remaining superfluities, grain by grain. And so with astronomy. Great lumps of error fell away in the lifetime of the first public astronomers; but the outline of a satisfactory method of navigation by the stars still failed to appear. The moon, "the inconstant moon," had still to be watched through many a weary revolution, and nearly a century passed away before the image in the rock at which the patient laborers had been so long toiling, could be distinctly traced. Not till near the close of that long period, had astronomy presented to the world a method of ocean longitude, within the outside limits specified by the parliamentary act of 1714. If, then, to make but a modest approach toward theoretic perfection, when practical astronomy was yet on every side open to easy improvement by the first comers, was a labor arduous and slow, what must have since been, what must yet continue to be, the toilsomeness of the task of working out its still higher improvement, and carrying it onward toward that standard of ideal perfection, which science will continue to approximate while the world stands, but after all, will never fully attain.

It is sometimes made our reproach, it is spoken of as if it were a preposterous thing, that we should desire to see Mississippi, as well as the rest of the world, doing something to promote the progress of this great work. Surely they upon whom the responsibility of the undertaking must fall, cannot be supposed to have any selfish feeling to gratify, any personal interests to serve, in urging this thing. To those to whom such an impression may have occurred, it would be instructive, if it were possible to observe an astronomer at his work. It is no child's play which occupies him. In the long, deep silence of the world's repose, sleepless himself though weary, fixed motionless in attitudes often painful, with an attention which must never flag, and an eye which must never relax its strain, he watches for hours the monotonous stars as they pass; and automatically, as if he were a part of the instrument which he controls, notes down the moment of their passage with the electric key. Night after night he follows up this unvarying and uninteresting toil. Day after day he elaborates the results with a lavish profusion of numerical computations, which leave the labors of the banker's clerk and accountant far in the shade. And this work, prosecuted for some years, enables him at last, perhaps to say that he has contributed his share toward removing one more small chip from the block in which the ideal perfection is still locked up. The picture may excite admiration; but certainly, seen from this point of view, there is nothing in it to invite emulation, or to promise ease. We admire, as we admire the elaborators of lexicons, and of concordances to the Holy Scriptures. And when we see one man after another devoting his strength to this exhausting work, and wearing himself out in the patient scrutiny of the starry heavens, instead of regarding him as an idle squanderer of the time and talents that God has given him, ought we not to look upon him rather, as truly as we do on Galileo himself, as belonging to the number of those whom science may justly rank in her noble army of martyrs!

The fact that the state of refinement which practical astronomy has attained to-day is such, that the observations of to-night cannot be turned to immediate account to-morrow morning, but that the accumulated results of many observations are necessary to a single additional step of progress, is one which places the science at a great disadvantage, when its claims are canvassed in the world. The incidental facts of discovery, therefore, which astronomers occasionally pick up, and which are of a nature to be generally understood, though they illustrate in no manner the great and proper labors of these useful men, are often seized upon by those who ignorantly depreciate the value of astronomical research, as if they were appropriate examples of the objects and ends of all modern astronomy. A telescopic comet is announced, and the discoverer is rewarded, perhaps, by a royal medal. Now, what of this comet? says the objector, and how is the world the better for its discovery? Well; for the present, we allow that we have nothing to say of the comet. We freely admit that we shall sleep no warmer in our beds, nor wake any richer in the morning, on account of it. Yet the reward is a just reward for vigilance, and vigilance certainly is valuable. Experience has, moreover, shown that the observation even of comets has no slight interest in its relations to the theory of gravitation, to the physical condition of the realms of space, and to the permanence of the system to which we belong. But let the comet go; class it with the Antarctic continent discovery by Wilkes, or with the boomerang of his Fejee islanders. We are not at all the happier or the less happy for the one or for the other; yet the Antarctic continent is, after all, a great fact; and the boomerang is a small one, which there was surely no harm in recording.

The objector sometimes, however, unconsciously founds his strictures upon discoveries which are not trifles. The undersigned has heard the question gravely raised, what advantage has the world derived from the discovery of the planet Uranus? The fact, remarks the objector, is called an important one; and yet, for nearly six thousand years according to Usher, mankind had got along very well without it. Now, this latter remark, be it observed, is very little to the purpose. Mankind got along well enough for a time without buttons and without breeches; and much longer without the printing press, and without the steam-engine. Mankind felt no need of cannon when there was no gunpowder, or of telegraph posts when there was no galvanism. Mankind got along very well without Uranus, and could have got on much longer under the same privation, had not Uranus been discovered. But to say that the discovery has been of no use,—this is an admission which we are not prepared to make. It has been of use, as may be easily illustrated.

First, however, let attention be drawn to an analogous discovery of somewhat later date, the history of which, both curious and instructive, may best precede what relates to Uranus. On the first day of January, of the year 1801, the very first day of the nineteenth century, the distinguished astronomer, Piazzi, of Palermo, observed a minute planet, never before noticed by human eye, since known by the name of Ceres. Compared with Uranus, it is but a sand-grain to a mountain. Compared even with our moon, it is but an insignificant globule—a pepper-corn to an orange. Yet its discovery had a value. Piazzi silently observed it, designing, so soon as he should have satisfactorily determined its orbit, to surprise the world by the announcement of a new member of the solar system; but it soon plunged into the overwhelming blaze of the solar radiance, and was lost to view for months. Unable, from the few observations he had gathered, to determine the path of the stranger, Piazzi at length laid the observations themselves before the astronomical world. The period of the probable emergence of the body from its veil of light having arrived, innumerable telescopes were directed toward the region of the heavens in which its track was presumed to lie; but not all the scrutiny nor all the perseverance of all the astronomers of Europe could suffice to recover the lost planet again to human view. Gradually a suspicion began to be whispered that the pretended discovery was no discovery at all; but that Piazzi had fabricated the observations with the malicious design to puzzle and annoy his contemporaries.

Now, at about this very period, a mathematician of Germany had had his thoughts turned toward a defect in the existing state of astronomical science, in regard to the determination of planetary paths. While this defect continued, it was impossible to test the question whether the observations were genuine or not. The occasion stimulated him to supply the defect; and the result, the "*Theoria Motus Corporum Cœlestium*" of Gauss, was one of the most valuable contributions to mathematical science ever made. By the aid of the "*Theoria Motus*," the path of the planet Ceres was traced from the time when it escaped from the hands of Piazzi. Gauss said to the astronomers, "Look yonder, and you will find your truant star." They looked, and the little globule was recovered on the first clear night thereafter.

Now, what the planet Ceres did for the world was, to improve mathematical science—the science whose useful applications on the earth are infinitely varied, and without which all our knowledge of the heavens derived from mere observation, would be of no value whatever, either to navigation or to any other end. And what the planet Ceres did, that the planet Uranus has done in a different manner.

From an early period following its discovery, this planet had been a very burthen upon the patience of astronomers, and a sore trial to their faith. From its motions as actually observed, its prospective motions as they ought to be, were deduced by computation; and its path was prescribed to it with a confidence which the tested power of physical astronomy had rendered somewhat strongly assured. But Uranus seemed very little to heed the dictates of the astronomers, and the path which they assigned him was one in which he chose not to walk. Moreover, after his discovery, the fact presented itself that he had already been observed nineteen times before, without being recognized as a planet—once so long before as 1690; and that when the positions which he occupied at the times of those ancient observations were compared with what they should have been according to the law of his later motion, there was a disagreement to an extent so large as to make it impossible to assign any path whatever to this contumacious planet, which should at the same time recognize the theory of gravitation, and harmonize the old observations with the new. Here was a case of real perplexity. It brought directly up the question whether or not the law of gravitation is, after all, one which can be universally relied on. Evidently the decision must go against the law, unless it can be shown that some disturbing body heretofore overlooked, exists within the limits of the system, and of which we know nothing now except what we read in the seeming caprices of Uranus. The data on which the discussion of this question was to proceed were evidently very slight—much slighter than had existed when Gauss attacked the problem of Ceres. Ceres had been seen—the unknown disturber of Uranus, never. But as if to illustrate the truth that, as difficulties accumulate, human energies correspondingly rise to their encounter, it was this time not a single champion who rushed forward to the support of troubled science, but two simultaneously, who, with equal enthusiasm, equal perseverance, and equal final success, attacked the difficulty, and bore off the plaudits of the world. Leverrier wrote to his friend at Berlin, "Examine the point I describe, and you will find the disturber." Galle turned his telescope in that direction, and in the self-same hour, Neptune was found. Simultaneously, Adams laid his finger on the map of the heavens, and said to the astronomer of Cambridge, "It is in this lurking-place, precisely, that you will find the author of all our confusion." The astronomer, Challis, distrusting isolated observations, commenced a systematic sweep of the whole region. He saw and recorded the planet twice without knowing it; and failed to make the discovery simply because he deferred the comparison of his observations until too late. Thus the benefit which has resulted ultimately to the world from the discovery of Uranus, is analogous to that of which Ceres was the occasion: it has wonderfully stimulated the ingenuity of men in the improvement of mathematical methods, and has thus contributed to the advancement of that science, without which no other exact science can exist.

It is hard, however, to be compelled to rest the argument for utility upon so narrow a basis as this. It is hard not to be permitted to think it useful, and as a lesson to human conceit valuable, to know that the insignificant ball on which we dwell is really, after all, not a very great nor a very magnificent portion of God's vast creation, or even of the planetary system to which it immediately belongs; that minute and insignificant as it appeared in the circle of its sister planets before the discovery of Uranus, its dignity was doubly dwarfed in consequence of that discovery, by the expansion of the system to twice its previously ascertained colossal dimensions, and has been a second time reduced in the same proportion, by the more recent discovery of Neptune.

And besides all this, it is really both annoying and discouraging to think that it seems not to be permitted to the hard-working and pains-taking astronomer to discover any thing for which he cannot find an immediately practical use, into the advantages of which all the world, learned and unlearned alike, can at once enter. What if there were no use in the occasional discovery of a planet or a comet, beyond the gratification it affords to the astronomical world? Is not that enough? Does not the astronomer render, in a thousand other ways, service enough to mankind to warrant his occasional indulgence in the luxury of a new planet? "Thou shalt not muzzle the ox when he treadeth out the corn," was the humane command of the Levitical law. If astronomy is of service to the world, at least let the world permit to the astronomer some sources of enjoyment from the results of his own labors.

In addition to the general considerations thus far presented, the undersigned now begs leave to offer a few specific arguments in favor of the project which he has had the honor, in the earlier portion of this letter, to submit to the enlightened deliberation of your honorable body.

I. In the first place, the existence of a school of higher learning in Mississippi is of essential importance in view of the instrumentality of such institutions in the development of native genius. There is no doubt that, among every people, there exist capacities that, for want of opportunity, are never developed. There is no doubt, that favoring opportunity has been the immediately stimulating cause of nearly all the greatness which the world ever saw. If the names of Washington and Greene, and Hancock and Jefferson, will forever ring in the ears of the human race, it is no doubt to the opportunity opened to them by the American Revolution, that their celebrity is to be ascribed. If the gigantic name of Napoleon fills up all the earlier years of the nineteenth century, it is no doubt to the opportunity presented to the youthful soldier by the command of the army of Italy, that his rapid march to empire is mainly attributable. There is probably not an ancient churchyard in the world, to which the expressive lines of Gray may not be appropriately applied:—

"Perhaps in this neglected spot is laid
Some heart once pregnant with celestial fire;
Hands which the rod of empire might have swayed
Or waked to ecstasy the living lyre.

"*But knowledge to their eyes her ample page,*
Rich with the spoils of time, did ne'er unroll—"

Ah, there the poet has touched the heart of the secret! Knowledge, indeed, is the potent instrumentality, after all, most essential to draw out the latent capabilities of the soul. For lack of knowledge many a Sheridan, unconscious of his powers, may have gone down voiceless to his grave; many a Milton, "mute and inglorious," may have passed away without a song; possibly, many a Newton, though the world has known but one, may have innocently held all his life the Ptolemean philosophy; and many a Brahe, or a Bessel, or a Herschel, may have attained to no greater intimacy with the stars of heaven than was enjoyed by the Chaldean shepherds whom they "gladdened on their mountain tops," in their solitary night-watches. If there is native genius in Mississippi, how without knowledge, here any more than elsewhere, can that genius waken into activity, ripen into strength, soar into celebrity? And if the opportunity is not here offered for the attainment of that knowledge which is so necessary to distinction, how or where shall it be obtained?

It is no reply to say that philosophers have sprung up independently of schools; and have grown famous without the aid of masters. The surface of the scientific field has been long since skimmed; and the original, unaided, and unschooled investigator must begin always at the surface. When the gold lies in nuggets, exposed to view, the first adventurer may pick it up and make it his own. The Chaldean could sit upon his hill-top, and become an astronomer as he watched his flock. From Hipparchus to Tycho Brahe, instrumental observation, though it had created the science anew, continued to be of the rudest kind, and anybody might employ it. Since Brahe's time, such has been the progress of improvement, that to-day, no man can become a practical astronomer, except within the walls of a regular observatory. There may be those who believe that, if we *have* youth among us of scientific tastes, and scientific ambitions, it is of no sort of importance whether they be drawn out and encouraged to labor for distinction to themselves and to their native State or not. With such, the undersigned can hold no argument, since the parties have no common ground on which to meet. The value, no less to a people than to individuals, of an honorable reputation, must be admitted, or every discussion, involving any but the most mercenary motives of action, must fall to the ground.

Will it, then, be said that the sources of the knowledge which has been represented as so valuable, will not be wanting to the ambitious aspirant, even though Mississippi should fail to furnish it? Will it be said that other States and other institutions have already made the provision which is here demanded; and that our youth may enjoy all the advantages which can be desired, without subjecting us to additional expense? The remark is sufficiently true as to its facts; but is not by any means so as to its inferences. The aspirant for scientific distinction can, it is admitted, seek sources of information elsewhere, after he begins to aspire; but what we want are the instrumentalities by which his aspirations are to be awakened. The benefits of distant institutions may be enjoyed by those who will go to a distance to find them; but, none will go who have no previously excited interest in the thing they seek.

Will it again be objected that, after all, there can be but few at most, who will devote themselves with ardor to the pursuit of high learning, or the prosecution of profound investigation—too few to deserve that we should make a special provision for them. The objection in its premises will be once more admitted without hesitation; but the justice or reasonableness of its conclusion will be wholly denied. Were all men to become philosophers, there would be no philosophers; were all men to become learned, there would be no learned men. Who does not remember, and who does not feel, the deep wisdom of the remark of the judicious and liberal-minded Huger, of South Carolina, on occasion of a powerful vindication before the legislature of that State, by the youthful M'Duffie, of the college which educated him—a remark which has not been so often repeated but that it will bear repetition again: "Had the college," said Judge Huger, "never done the State a single service except to educate that young man, she would have made an ample return for all the money that has ever been lavished on her." If any thing is needed to dispose of the objection thus suggested, it may be found in the spirit of this observation. Comment would only weaken the argument.

It is held, then, that the measures of higher development to which it is proposed that the University of Mississippi should now begin to conform her policy, will be attended with at least one recognizable, tangible, definable advantage. Let us inquire whether there be no other.

II. Throughout the entire South, for the past twenty years, and in the years immediately preceding the present, with an intensity constantly growing, we have heard continually the demand earnestly uttered in every quarter, that Southern youth should be educated in Southern institutions of learning. From the press, from the platform, from the pulpit, from the legislative benches, and from the executive chair, in our own and in every neighboring State, one unanimous and emphatic expression of opinion on this subject has proceeded, each confirming and strengthening the rest, and altogether forming a solid and compact mass of public sentiment which cannot be mistaken. And the public sentiment is right. If we had no peculiar interests to render the home education of our youth specially important to us, it would unquestionably be the part of the highest wisdom to rear up our youth to manhood among the scenes with which they are to be in life identified. The ulterior value of early acquaintances and of the ties of college friendship, is too great to be thrown indifferently away, as it is thrown away to every useful purpose when a youth is educated a thousand miles from his home, unless in view of some great countervailing advantage.

Few Southern parents can be found, who are not ready to admit the truth of all this. And yet a great many Southern parents are found, who still send their children away, not merely to other Southern States, but to New Jersey, to New York, and to New England. What reason shall be assigned for this? Is there any describable benefit which these parents expect to secure, by a measure so in conflict with public sentiment all about them? And if there is, is there any benefit sufficient to countervail the great and obvious evil of foregoing home influences, destroying home associations, renouncing home friendships? Certainly they believe that there is; and this advantage they believe that they find in superior institutions, and superior means and appliances for the communication of knowledge. Is their belief correct?

If we trust the testimony of our presses, if we yield credit to the expressed convictions of our fellow-citizens on every side, we shall be slow to admit that there are anywhere to be found educational advantages superior to those which we possess. Not a public exhibition can be held in any Southern college, not a public examination can take place in any Southern school, without eliciting a volume of delighted and exultant praise, which exhausts the vocabulary of panegyric, and leaves the enthusiastic commentator and critic at a loss for words. We have no such thing as a second-rate school among us. We have no such thing as a school with its strong points and its weak points. All our schools are strong —they have no weak points. Their strength is capable of expression only in the superlative degree; they are superlative in general excellence, and all their parts, their departments, their operations, their accommodations, their apparatus and their *personnel* are superlative also. Our system is the wisest system, our discipline is the most judicious discipline, our Faculties are the ablest Faculties, and our scholars are the very most proficient scholars, the world ever saw. To sum up all in one grand expressive word—our *advantages*—a term of convenient comprehensiveness, into the meaning of which it is well not too curiously to inquire,—our advantages surpass by far all ever before offered, in any age of the world, or in any community, to the appreciative patronage of an enlightened public.

This can hardly be called a caricature. Scarcely a word or sentence has been employed, of which the counterpart may not be found in the columns of the Southern press, *passim;* and as to the sentiment of the whole, it is the most familiar of all that salute our ears. Who ever heard of a college or a school of any pretensions within our borders, which was *not* all that is here described? Now, the total absence of every thing like a discriminating, or appreciative, or just mode of dealing with the claims and merits of our institutions of learning, on the part of those who undertake to direct public opinion, is pernicious in a variety of ways. It checks in the institutions themselves the spirit of improvement; since if they can so cheaply win the guerdon of superlative praise, they will hardly think it worth their while to labor for a substantial merit which nobody appreciates. It misleads, most unhappily, the public mind, by producing a contented faith in a merit which is in too many cases, more imaginary than real; and thus averting from the institutions that outside pressure, which is the most effectual stimulus to internal improvement. But, finally, *it is clearly seen through* by the well-educated and intelligent, and dispassionately judging among ourselves; who, disgusted with hyperbole, and anxious for a little honest fact, send, therefore, their children to distant institutions, of long-standing and undoubted character; reconciling themselves, as well as they can, to the unwelcome necessity, by the consideration that if their children are denied the benefit of an education at home, they will at least enjoy the benefit of an education.

But, after all, have we no institutions capable of thoroughly educating our own youth upon our own soil? It is not the undersigned who has assumed so broad a ground as that we have not. It is only those Southern parents who, bewildered by the system of universal laudation which prevails among us, are unable to discover whether we have or not; and so cut the knot at once, by withholding their patronage equally from all. But dismissing for a moment the question here raised, in so far as it relates to that branch of education which has been distinguished as disciplinary, it is an opinion which the undersigned is compelled to entertain, that, in regard to all that relates to the second, or doctrinal, branch, there is not at present—unless by the enlightened action of your honorable body, within the last two years, an exception may be fairly assumed to have been created here—an institution of learning in all the South, which can justly claim for itself an undeniable equality of merit with any one of several of the older colleges of the North; much less one entitled to arrogate to itself superlatives of praise.

To you, Gentlemen, is certainly to be awarded high honor for your distinct perception of these things, and for the energetic measures which you have taken, and are still taking, to remove one Southern institution at least from the sweeping category. It is not, therefore, to you that the undersigned feels bound to apologize for the plainness of his speech. To his fellow-citizens he would say that if the language here held is more novel than complimentary, this is only because, in order that we may mend our deficiencies, it is necessary first that we should look them distinctly in the face.

What, then, is it which leads so many Southern parents to prefer Northern institutions to their own? If there is difference of merit, in what does the difference consist? All the educational advantages which institutions of learning present to seekers after knowledge, must be traceable to one or other of the three following heads: 1. The personal ability of teachers; 2. The material and instrumental means and appliances auxiliary to instruction; and 3. The methods. The third and last of these heads may be at once dismissed, since the practical methods of instruction in all our colleges, instrumental illustrations apart, are so similar that the consideration of methods of instruction is rarely the determining one in the mind of a parent. The first deserves to be dwelt on a little more maturely. The personal reputation of a teacher highly distinguished for his attainments in letters or science, not seldom weighs much in a question of this kind; but when we consider in how many of our colleges, from Virginia to Louisiana, there are really teachers of eminent ability, well-known learning, or profound science, we must be satisfied that it is not here that we are to look for the solution of our present difficulty.

What then remains, if it be not the imperfect provision which exists in so many of our colleges, as compared with those in the North to which Southern youth chiefly resort, in regard to the material and instrumental means of imparting knowledge mainly upon subjects of physical and chemical science, of geology, mineralogy and natural history, all of them matters esteemed, in the present age of the world, to possess a high practical value, and of which, under the galloping system of teaching already abundantly signalized in this letter, it is only by the aid of the most ample illustration that any thing can be really taught at all.

There need be no hesitancy in saying that our Southern colleges, as a class, are in this respect generally deficient. They may occupy eligible locations; they may possess learned and able teachers; in what relates to mental training and discipline—to education, in short, in the proper and literal sense of that word—they may be entitled to all the praise they claim; but, as to the second branch of their business, as to *instruction*, as distinguished from education, and as to their means of making it clear, comprehensive, and thorough—their libraries, their philosophical and chemical apparatus their collections illustrative of the mineral, vegetable, and animal kingdoms,—as to these things, the contrast between them and those richly endowed and venerable, institutions which so many Southern parents prefer, is so glaring as to throw itself upon our notice, whether we will regard it or not.

What is the remedy? Not denunciation, surely—not reproach—not crimination. No! Instead of all this, it is to throw around our own institutions precisely the same attractions, and without any exception all the attractions, which exist elsewhere to draw our youth away. It will cost money—true; but then the money will be well expended. From a pretty extensive examination of college catalogues, the undersigned is prepared to believe that not fewer than two hundred Mississippi youth are now constantly pursuing their education beyond the limits of the State; many of them, it is true, in Southern colleges, but colleges supposed to be better provided than ours with the instrumentalities necessary to the satisfactory presentation of subjects of physical science. The offer of sufficient counter-attractions here, may reasonably be presumed likely to detain hereafter at least one hundred of this number at home. Now, the education of every such student may, without extravagance, be estimated to cost—tuition, and living, and clothing, and books, and travelling to and fro, to say nothing of pocket expenditures, being included—not less than six hundred dollars per annum; so that a total sum of one hund ed and twenty thousand dollars is annually raised in Mississippi and expended abroad, of which one half at least might be just as well retained at home.

And this sum, if not more, as a consequence of the judicious, and thoughtful, and far-seeing policy which has prompted the expenditure of a much less considerable amount in strengthening the University of Mississippi in the point where strength has been most needed, probably will in coming years be saved to the State. Having brought into so strong relief, what is believed to be the principal cause of the want of popularity of Southern colleges with Southern men, the undersigned would commit an unpardonable oversight, were he not to express his conviction that this University is, to-day, in possession of a philosophical and chemical apparatus as a whole without a superior on the continent, and in many of its details unequalled; that it possesses a mineral collection of which the rare beauty of the specimens is rivalled only in the richest cabinets of the country; and that in conchology it has a treasure to which no similar institution in the United States can present a parallel. Much of what is here described, though provided by your own order, has not yet been presented to your inspection. At your next assembling, you will have the satisfaction of seeing one Southern college, which, in regard to the most important and popular branches of physical science, will present every attraction to the learner which can be offered by the oldest and best appointed in the entire country.

Astronomy yet remains to be provided for. That portion of the plan of improvement sanctioned at your meeting in July, 1856, which relates to this science, has as yet but imperfectly been carried into execution. Your observatory remains incomplete, and instruments for observation remain unprovided. Now, whatever may be the opinions men may entertain in regard to the importance of creating facilities for forming an acquaintance with the heavens in connection with our colleges, however superciliously men may regard practical astronomy for its own sake, nobody can deny that the possession of such facilities does actually contribute to the consideration in which the institutions where they exist are held; nobody can deny that they are really attractions which exercise a powerful influence upon the imagination, and that they are positively effective in securing patronage. At the meeting of 1856, to which allusion has just been made, it is believed that every member of your honorable body who was present was fully satisfied of the correctness of this principle, viz: that whatever attractions, no matter of what kind, may exist elsewhere, to draw the youth of Mississippi away to institutions of learning foreign to the State, the same attractions ought to be created here, simply because they are attractions. It is believed that it was then admitted without controversy to be unnecessary to discuss in labored detail the intrinsic merits of every specific measure of improvement proposed, provided it could be said of it that it is a measure which other and distant colleges have adopted, and which is capable of being urged as evidence of the superiority of those institutions by citizens of our own State who choose to patronize them. Not that, by acting on this principle, we are really in danger of adopting any measure intrinsically useless; but that the principle affords a short cut to a good and sufficient reason for what we do, and sets aside the necessity for many and weary words.

Now, from the manner in which the measures proposed here in regard to practical astronomy have been spoken of by some, one would imagine it to be an unprecedented thing for a college in the United States to possess an observatory. And yet there are nearly a dozen American colleges fully provided in this respect, in most or all of which active observation is constantly kept up; and among the number are three or four possessing instruments which rank among the most magnificent in the world. Nothing is aimed at in the University of Mississippi more than all these colleges have already done; and if the propriety of carrying out to completion the measures initiated in 1856, be rested on no higher ground than that of the self-interest which should prompt us to endeavor to clothe ourselves with all the attractions which other institutions possess, further argument would seem to be unnecessary.

At any rare, it is quite undeniable that there is but one way in which we can put ourselves entirely in the right, when we demand of Southern parents that they shall educate their sons at home; and that is by following out the policy indicated above, no matter to what results it may lead us, no matter what measures it may force upon us. So long as we leave any opening whatever for such parents to say that we fail to provide here the advantages, and all the advantages, which can be found elsewhere, so long we must refrain from reproaching them if they see fit to resist the temptations we do really lay before them, and still pass us by to prefer the North.

There remain two further considerations only, which the undersigned desires, before concluding, to suggest as matters of reflection. One of these has rèference to our feelings of honorable pride; the other, to our sense of duty.

III. And first, as to our pride. We certainly cannot but desire that the institution in which we all of us feel so deep an interest shall not only accomplish a good and useful work, but that it shall build up for itself an honorable and enviable reputation. There is not a Mississippian anywhere, in whom it would not excite a feeling of proud exultation to hear the University of the State of which he is a citizen, spoken of by people at a distance in terms of respect and admiration. It is folly to affect contempt for a consideration of this kind. When character losesits value in the minds of men, the basis of all motive to improvement, the stimulus to all honorable aspiration, is swept away. The love of approbation is implanted in our natures by God himself; and so long as those natures remain unchanged, so long will it be a legitimate argument in favor of any act or any measure, that it is adapted to secure the good opinions of mankind.

Now, the only infallible mode of acquiring an honorable reputation, and a reputation which shall be not only honorable but permanent, is to deserve it. And our desert is measured not merely by the degree of our well-doing in that which we do, but also no less by the loftiness of our aims, and the magnitude of our attempts. If we confine our views to the comparatively humble object of training boyish intellects, and do this faithfully and successfully, we shall have accomplished a good work, and have entitled ourselves to be well spoken of; but our reputation will correspond with the grade of our labor, and will hardly overpass the boundaries of our own State. But if our ambitions are more aspiring, and we aim to satisfy the cravings of maturer minds; if, not content with an humble station in the vestibule of the temple of science, we pass the sublime portals, and plant ourselves as ministers at the radiant shrine itself,—then, if our success be in any manner proportioned to our daring, we shall have accomplished a much greater work than the former, and have assured to ourselves a wider consideration, which it depends only on ourselves to exalt into celebrity. Of this fact we may be well assured, that the attention of men will be drawn to us just in proportion as the level on which we choose to plant ourselves is more elevated. In this respect there is an analogy between moral and material things. That object is ever most conspicuous whose position is highest. A city in a valley may easily be overlooked; but the city which is set on a hill cannot be hid.

Nor must we overlook the reflex influence upon the

instructor himself which must be consequent upon increasing the dignity of his task. In the ordinary routine of collegiate instruction, there is little to stimulate the teacher to self-improvement, or to inspire him with the ambition to make larger attainments than are necessary to fit him for the business of conducting the daily examinations of the recitation-room. It has already been pointed out in what manner the system of college instruction which depends on examination exclusively, tends to repress the properly teaching spirit; it may be added, as a circumstance no less to be lamented, that it actually furnishes a screen to the deficiencies of the teacher. There is indeed no disposition to deny that an honest and conscientious man who feels himself deficient, may endeavor to improve, out of a mere sense of duty. It is, on the other hand, freely admitted that men may, if they will, be personally as proficient under one system as under another; but all this does not make it the less true that men in every situation are influenced by circumstances, as well as by principle and the sense of duty; that different systems do not equally stimulate men to effort; and that, in the long run, it will generally be found—a consequence probably of the weakness of human nature—that the aggregate of performance in the discharge of duty is proportioned more to the force of external influences than to the weight of moral obligation. In proportion as the duty of the instructor is of higher grade, in proportion as it involves the necessity of larger attainments, in the same proportion he must himself rise, and the comprehensiveness of his knowledge must be wider. And if at the same time the system of instruction to which he is obliged to conform be such that, instead of permitting him to act the part of a mere listener to the performances of his pupils, it compels him to be himself the living expositor of his subject, then he is brought under the influence of the highest stimulus to exertion by which a man in his position can possibly be actuated, the ambition to attain an honorable personal reputation; an ambition secretly reinforced by the consciousness that to be deficient is to incur inevitable exposure, and that to be exposed is to be disgraced.

Nor in vindicating the policy of aiming to elevate the grade of teaching in the University of Mississippi, are we without an argument of a more utilitarian, or, as it may perhaps be called, a more mercenary character. If it is true that, in thus elevating our aims, we may reasonably hope to secure for the institution a higher, a more honorable, and a more extended reputation, it cannot but be anticipated, as a necessary consequence, that the number of those who resort here for instruction will correspondingly increase. In this consideration we may find a justification, not merely of the measure now immediately under discussion, but of every measure of improvement, and of every expenditure of every kind, which creates here a new attraction to counteract those other attractions which are continually drawing the youth of Mississippi to distant colleges

The undersigned is well aware with how grave misgivings the expenditures made for the sake of improving the internal efficiency of colleges, and their general attractiveness to students, are often regarded by outside observers. But really such expenditures are among the most judicious investments that can possibly be made; and sooner or later they infallibly pay for themselves. A slight permanent increase of the number of students will in due time reimburse the treasury for a large expenditure; a larger increase will do it sooner; and when it is done, the objects of the investment will become a permanent addition to the capital, while the income will be increased by a perpetual annuity. Suppose, for example, one thousand dollars to be applied in some such way as to be a means of adding a single student to each class in college. Form the annual payments of these additional students, which are made at the beginning of each year in advance, into a sinking fund, and the debt with interest will be cancelled in five years; after which the revenue of the institution will be permanently increased about two hundred dollars per annum.

In speculating on a matter of this kind, we must consider that it is always quite impossible to say precisely what increase of number has been effected by any given measure of improvement, whether it be one which involves expenditure or not. But, on the other hand, when improvement is followed by increase of number, it is equally impossible to doubt the reality of a connection between the two events in the relation of cause and effect; and when this increase is considerable, it needs no very great arithmetical ability to demonstrate that the money it may have cost has been well laid out.

Nor need this assertion be deemed inconsistent with what has already been said, of the impossibility of sustaining colleges upon fees alone. It must be considered that there are certain large investments which must be made in the very beginning, in order that the college may exist. These are locked up in buildings and grounds, or take the form of foundations for professorships. Now, the number of students may very largely vary, without occasioning any material variation in the amount thus invested. If we suppose that all necessary buildings are provided, and that some of the officers, at least, are supported by the endowment, then the tuition fees constitute a fluctuating source of revenue, which may largely increase before there need be any material increase of expenditure. Hence, though it *is* a fact that collegiate education is furnished below its cost, this does not make it, as at first thought this statement might lead one to suppose, like other kinds of losing business, a source of larger loss in proportion as more of it is done. There is, on the other hand, at present rates of tuition, low as they are, a pecuniary advantage in having many students; and hence it is a wise economy which expends money in adding to the educational advantages offered by any institution of learning, since the inevitable result of such expenditures is to attract increase of patronage.

Thus far it has been argued, that the measure of improvement recommended in this communication will only react advantageously upon the reputation of the University, and thus secure certain specific advantages to the institution itself. But this is by no means all; the effect will not stop here, but will extend in a sensible degree to the people of the entire State. It is, in a great degree, through their institutions, that the characters of communities are judged. There is no institution in Mississippi, and evidently there can be none, whose aspect, in the eyes of distant observers, will ever present a more significant or decisive indication of the intelligence of our people, than that of this University. Whatever raises the character of the University, raises the State in the consideration of mankind. There are reasons why, in the nature of things, it must be so. The University, as the chief educational institution of the State, will ultimately determine the kind and grade of teaching in all other schools; and the popular enlightenment must always maintain a certain definite relation to the character of the schools in which the people are taught. Distant observers will judge of the invisible effect, by the visible cause. If the University stands high in a literary and scientific point of view, the inference is a natural one, that it cannot be other than an intelligent people whose educational training is subject to such a control. There is another mode of view-

ing the subject, from which the same inference may be drawn. Regarding the University not as acting upon the people, but as being acted upon by them, not as determining the popular character for intelligence, but as being determined in its own character by the popular will, it will follow no less than before, that precisely according as its own intellectual position is assumed at a higher or lower level, the repute in which the State itself is held abroad will also be higher or lower.

This topic is sufficiently fertile to warrant further expansion; but already this letter has reached an extent unanticipated, and larger than could have been desired. A few words only will therefore be added upon the remaining point.

IV. The measure of improvement proposed, recommends itself to our sense of duty. Whatever may be said of the value to mankind of this or that fact of scientific discovery, or of this or that achievement of literary genius, there can be no sort of doubt of the general truth that letters and science have actually made men both happier and better. If we extend our views no further than to what concerns the physical comfort of the race, it is undeniable that all the advancement the world has ever seen has been due first of all to mental improvement, and to the resulting conquests of mind over matter. Wide as is the interval which divides savage from civilized life, its existence is a living testimony to the power of cultivated intellect, of which exclusively it is the creation. Now, it is char-

acteristic of the triumphs of mind, that their resultant benefits to mankind are not restricted by any natural limitation to specific localities or, to particular peoples. From the moment in which they are achieved, they are equally capable of contributing, and so far as the prejudices and perversity of the race will permit, they do immediately contribute, to the well-being of all nations, and the prosperity of all lands. It is, furthermore, a dictate of the sense of right and justice innate in every rational being, that the reception of benefits imposes on the recipient reciprocal obligations, which are morally if not legally binding. In return for the protection thrown around us by the civil and political institutions under which we live, no one questions that it is the duty of every citizen to contribute to the support of government; and in this case, as the security of society depends upon the fulfilment of the obligation, the coercive power of the law is employed to reinforce in men's minds the too often inoperative convictions of duty. Where there is less at stake, or where it is less easy to point out specifically what and how much it belongs to each individual to do toward the discharge of a debt in which all are debtors, in such cases if the moral sense is not active enough to stimulate performance, the obligation remains unfulfilled. But in such cases it is far nobler to obey the promptings of duty, than in those in which the option is taken away; precisely as it is nobler to do right because it *is* right, than to do it because it is a necessity.

And in precisely this condition are all communities of men everywhere, in regard to and in consequence of the benefits which they have derived from the softening influence of letters in ameliorating manners, and the all but creative power of science in improving arts. The obligation rests upon every people who have been partakers of the vast advantages which flow from intellectual illumination, to do something on their own part to feed the flame whose light has shone so gloriously for them. It becomes, in short, a high-minded people to manifest the existence within itself of a sentiment loftier than that of the sluggish selfishness which accepts without hesitation and enjoys without scruple whatever creative genius has produced of beautiful or useful, yet never on its own part aspires to create, or seeks to contribute to the potential sources of human happiness.

Would a people fulfil its duties to mankind growing out of the considerations here succinctly presented, it is not to be done by a personal contribution to the great fund of literary or scientific treasures which make up the intellectual wealth of the world, on the part of each individual member of society. Enough has been already said to show, that in the existing state of the world's advancement, it is no longer in the power of the occasional student or of the casual observer, to forward to any material degree the progress of either literary or scientific improvement. The devotion of long years of faithful industry is necessary to an adequate understanding of the existing condition of the field of labor; and evidently no champion can be in position to attack the unknown with success, until he shall have made himself first master of the known. Therefore it is, that the debt which every enlightened people owe to the world, in return for the benefits which they themselves have received at the hands of science and good learning, can only be repaid by creating the instrumentalities which shall raise up among themselves scientific and learned men. Such men, entering the field of original and independent investigation, may give back to the world at least a modest tribute of newly discovered truth, in return for the inestimable treasure of accumulated knowledge which they have received; and in doing this they will at the same time draw down imperishable honor on the people by whom their genius has been stimulated to activity, and on the land which their labors have made illustrious.

Is it possible that the people of Mississippi do not recognize the obligation which it is attempted here, imperfectly and feebly, to explain and to bring into relief? Shall we, too, illustrate anew to the world the truth of the tyrant's dogma, that letters wither, that science perishes, beneath the mephitic breath of republican institutions? Shall it continue forever to be the reproach of civil liberty, the opprobrium and scandal of democratic governments, that they are unfavorable to the advancement of the race in all that constitutes its truest grandeur and glory?

There are pleas, it is not forgotten, by which it is

attempted to evade or break the force of appeals like these. Mississippi, it is said, is still in her infancy; and it cannot be expected of her that she should undertake labors such as have marked the history of other communities only in the maturity of their powers. But in this reasoning there lurks a certain fallacy, which destroys all its force. Considered as a political organization, Mississippi is indeed an infant State; but in so far as the word infancy as applied to nations is understood to imply recent emergence from barbarism, or a present feeble diffusion of intellectual light, Mississippi is not infant. The bulk of the actual population of this State consisted in the beginning, as a great portion of it still consists, of natives of the older States situated upon the Atlantic coast, whose origin dates back to times antecedent to the American Revolution. It was not a class of ignorant and needy adventurers who planted themselves upon these fertile river valleys, and laid here the broad foundations of a future magnificent State. They were intelligent and enlightened men, many of them highly educated, some of them wealthy, nearly all of them in comfortable circumstances. They left behind them nowhere a community more respectable in an intellectual point of view, than they themselves constituted here. Nor has Mississippi retrograded. If the sons of her immigrant citizens have not always found education at home, they have found education. And therefore, if the State is really infant in point of intellectual development, to the extent that she may fairly plead her infancy in bar of the just claims of the world upon her, then the whole continent is infant, and all America is entitled to equal immunity from the pressure of similar obligations.

Neither can Mississippi be said to be infant in point of resources. Already among the foremost of the producing States of the Union, and annually increasing the amount of her production with a rapidity outrunning all preconceived anticipation, she is at this moment, regard being had to her numerical population, one of the richest states in the world. Moreover, if this were not true, the question immediately in discussion relates not to the diversion of any part of the wealth of Mississippi herself to the encouragement of literary advancement or of scientific discovery; but only to the wisest and best mode of applying a fund of origin foreign to the State, held by Mississippi in trust for the educational benefit of her own sons.

Another objection, however, is sometimes raised. It is said that the entire educational system of the State is at present in a condition of very imperfect efficiency, and is almost destitute of any consistent organization. Under these circumstances, it is urged, with some plausibility, as the dictate of expediency, that we waive for the moment the claims of the higher education, until we shall have made ample, or at least adequate, provision for the lower. No citizen of the State is a more ardent advocate, or a more zealous friend, of the cause of popular education than the undersigned. But it is for this very reason that he advocates, first of all, the perfection of the institutions of the highest learning. It is only through the instrumentality of these, that the schools of inferior grade can be made efficient. If schools without any teachers at all would be good for nothing, then schools with teachers themselves of inferior scholarship and a limited range of attainments are not much better. It would therefore be but idle legislation which should provide, no matter how liberally, for the support of schools, and should fail to provide at the same time for the education of teachers. Now, in a *prima-facie* view of the case, two circumstances present themselves which apparently break the force of this argument; yet which, on closer examination, only serve to confirm it. The first is, that teachers of merit are often actually found to take charge of the primary and secondary schools in States in which, as in past years in Mississippi, collegiate institutions have not existed in sufficient number, or on a scale sufficiently enlarged, to supply them; and the second grows out of the circumstance that the teachers of the most numerous class of schools—the common schools, as they are called—are not usually formed directly by the colleges, but by the schools of secondary grade. As to the first of these facts, observation will show that the teachers not made by ourselves and for ourselves, but who appear to be thus made to our hand, are teachers who have been formed in the schools of higher learning in other States, many of them in distant States, and who have come among us because they perceived an advantageous field to be here open. This supply of educational assistance is evidently precarious in its character, and without any guaranty for its uniformity of merit or consistency of practice. More than this, if there be any who can believe that it is in keeping with the proper dignity of a great and wealthy State like Mississippi, or with what is due to a just sense of self-respect in her, to depend on foreign aid for the supply of the first of her educational necessities, such persons take a view of the case which is entirely incompatible with the convictions of the undersigned.

As to the second of the facts above suggested, viz., that many teachers of the primary schools, perhaps the greater number, are not graduates of collegiate institutions, and as to the inference which is very frequently, and at first view not unnaturally, drawn from this circumstance, that the colleges have nothing to do with the grade of their scholarship,—if we consider that these teachers must nevertheless be formed somewhere, and that the schools in which they are formed must be in the hands of teachers of a higher order, who themselves must depend upon the colleges for their education, it will be evident that the reasoning which would make popular education on this account independent of the higher, is entirely fallacious. The conclusion is inevitable, that if we would have good common schools, we must first of all have good colleges. And if we would aim by legislation to elevate or depress, in the directest and most expeditious mode possible, the character of such common-school education as we have, we can accomplish this object in no other way so decisively as by exalting or degrading the character of the higher seminaries.

Now, beyond the objections which have been thus disposed of, it does not really appear that there exists any other capable of being even plausibly urged as a reason why Mississippi should not make some original contribution on her own part, to the world's advancement in letters and science. Why should she not? Is there any thing in her laws to fetter genius; in her climate to paralyze industry; in her public sentiment to discourage ambition? Or will it be urged in her behalf, as an excuse of her dearth of performance, that the intellect of her sons is unequal to the task of achieving for her an honorable name in the great republic of letters? Surely none of these things are true.

What, then, is the obvious dictate of duty? Is it not to build up here, upon a foundation already laid—the fittest foundation which could be selected in all our borders—of an institution of the highest learning—an institution, which, while it shall continue to discharge its present functions even more perfectly than ever heretofore, shall nevertheless lift its aims to that higher level, at which it may number, not immature youth only, but earnest men in the ranks of its scholars; and so stimulate the activity of native genius as presently to secure for Mississippi a recognized place among the positive promoters of the intellectual progress of the race?

If among the modes by which it has been proposed to enlist Mississippi in the service of science, astronomical observation has been early and prominently presented, this is because astronomical observation affords one of the most direct means of associating useful scientific labor here, with useful scientific labor in other parts of the country, and in other parts of the world. Practical astronomy is a science which continually opens out to itself new fields of labor, even while yet the ancient fields are far from being exhausted. Many subjects require a delicate, refined, and long-continued scrutiny, in which the associated efforts of many observatories have a peculiar value. Thus, at this moment, a series of observations upon the moon is going on in this country, originally suggested by Professor Bache, the able chief of the United States Coast Survey, in concert with the eminent physical astronomer of Harvard University, Prof. Peirce, in which the co-operation of all the observatories of the Union is invoked, and in reference to which computations made in advance for the meridian and latitude of Oxford, with maps of the phenomena as predicted for this place, have been forwarded from Washington to this University, at intervals, during the past eighteen months. Yet in this labor, in the unprovided state of the observatory of the University, it has not been permitted us to bear our part. Let the building but be completed, and the instruments contemplated in its plan be erected, and the University of Mississippi may become immediately and honorably associated with every other institution engaged in the promotion of astronomical science, and may shortly become familiarly known in every civilized land, as one of the noblest creations of the enlightened intelligence of modern times.

The task, Gentlemen, proposed to himself by the undersigned in the preparation of this letter, is ended. With whatever success it may appear in the event that he shall have succeeded in impressing his views upon your minds, he will ever carry with him that species of contentment which springs from the consciousness of having, according to the light within him, honestly discharged his duty to the Board who have honored him with their confidence, to the University in the prosperity of which he feels so deep an interest, and to the cause of education, in all its grades, throughout the State of Mississippi.

To your hands is committed, for the present generation at least, the moulding of the policy of this institution. Even though it should seem to you advisable still to restrict the University to the comparatively humble field of usefulness within which its operations have been hitherto confined, it will yet be a valuable institution, and one with which you may be justly proud that your names are to be forever associated. For this will be your noblest monument; and no matter in what other, and temporarily perhaps more brilliant, walks of life your services may have been or may be required by your State, you will leave behind you no record more permanently visible or more emphatically honorable than this. Political distinctions may fill up the present hour with idle parade, and call forth noisy applauses from unthinking crowds. If they have been or shall be yours, you may well afford to esteem lightly the reputation they leave; but it can never be without a feeling of the deepest satisfaction that you can look forward to that period in the distant future, when your children and your children's children shall find here a prouder memorial of your wisdom than all the boastful legends ever carved in brass or marble could afford; and pointing to the University, with an exultation which only the worthy descendants of worthy sires can fully comprehend, shall be able to say, "Behold! their works do praise them."

Should you, however, see fit, from this time forward to open to the University that higher sphere of labor and influence which it has been the object of this communication to suggest, there may be in reserve for it a future not only of usefulness but of renown; and to those whose wise discernment shall have enabled them, at this early day, to discover all the greatness and grandeur of its true mission, and whose judicious action shall have put in the way to fulfil its lofty destiny, posterity will award the homage of a still higher reverence. For grudgingly as a world too usually parsimonious where it should be liberal, and lavish where it should be frugal, may be disposed to contribute of its abundance for the encouragement of objects whose tendency is to elevate the race in point of intelligence and true dignity, it is yet, after all, not slow to appreciate that breadth of view and loftiness of aim which it is incapable of emulating; and it honors, at least with its applauses, though it may fail to load with its gifts, all who contribute directly or indirectly to the prosecution of the mighty conquests of the human understanding. Well, indeed, may it do so! For what are all the structures man can rear of polished marble or ponderous granite, in comparison with the grand and imperishable creations of the majestic intellect! And what though it be given but to few, by the force of native endowments or the energy of an indomitable perseverance, personally to assist in lifting to a loftier and still loftier height the proud temple which the conspiring labors of successive generations have reared to science in the midst of the nations, surely, no one of all mankind can be insensible to the sublimity of an edifice whose foundations are as broad as the boundaries of the earth, and whose vaulted dome is studded with the stars of heaven.

With the highest respect, Gentlemen,

Your obedient servant,

F. A. P. BARNARD.

www.ingramcontent.com/pod-product-compliance
Lightning Source LLC
LaVergne TN
LVHW021427110826
845150LV00007B/2118

* 9 7 8 1 4 2 5 5 0 7 3 1 2 *